WHEN CAN WE TALK?

WHEN CAN WE TALK?

A GUIDEBOOK FOR CAREGIVERS HOLDING DISCUSSIONS AROUND DIFFICULT TOPICS

FERN PESSIN

URBAN VILLA PRESS
SINCE 2019

Copyright © 2023 Fern Pessin. All rights reserved.

When Can We Talk? Copyright © 2023

No part of this publication shall be reproduced, transmitted, or sold in whole or in part in any form without prior written consent of the author, except as provided by the United States of America copyright law. Any unauthorized usage of the text without express written permission of the publisher is a violation of the author's copyright and is illegal and punishable by law. All trademarks and registered trademarks appearing in this guide are the property of their respective owners.

For permission requests, write to the publisher, addressed "Attention: Permissions Coordinator," at the address below.

Urban Villa Press
8326 Pineville Matthews Rd,
Ste 407-470522
Charlotte, NC 28226

Ordering Information: Quantity sales and special discounts are available on quantity purchases by corporations, associations, and others. For details, contact the publisher at the address above.

Edited by: Chris O'Byrne

Cover design by: Alex Valchev & Debbie O'Byrne
Typeset by: JETLAUNCH

Printed in Charlotte, NC in the United States of America

ISBN: 979-8-89079-047-7 (paperback)
ISBN: 979-8-89079-048-4 (ebook)

Library of Congress Control Number: 2023919326
First edition, November 2023.
The information in this book is for educational purposes only.

This publication contains the opinions and ideas of its author. It is intended to provide helpful and informative material on the subjects addressed in the publication. It is sold with the understanding that the author and publisher are not engaged in rendering medical, health, financial, legal, or any other kind of personal professional services in the book. The material may include information, products, or services by third parties. As such, the author and publisher do not assume responsibility or liability for any third-party material or opinions. Readers are advised to do their own due diligence when it comes to making decisions. The author and publisher specifically disclaim all responsibility for any liability, loss, or risk, personal or otherwise, which is incurred as a consequence, directly or indirectly, of the use and application of any of the information contained in this book.

Neither the author nor the publisher shall be liable or responsible for any loss or damage allegedly arising from any information included in this book. Nothing contained in this book is intended to be instructional for medical diagnosis or treatment. Nothing contained in this book is intended to be legal or financial advice for your personal situation. The information should not be considered complete, nor should it be relied on to suggest a course of treatment or actions for a particular individual. It should not be used in place of a visit, call, consultation, or the advice of your physician or other qualified healthcare provider, legal counsel, or financial advisor. Neither the author nor the publisher directly or indirectly practice medicine, therapy, dispense medical services, financial advising, or legal counsel as part of this book.

At the time of writing, all the URLs, addresses, phone numbers, and statistics are current. Please note that over time, information and/or access to certain pages may change.

Data and organizations mentioned within this book are primarily US-based. Financial and legal terms are based on the author's local knowledge and may be different in other countries and in different municipalities throughout the United States.

Some names and locations were changed to respect privacy.

I write this for all the people on this caregiving journey with me.

With gratitude to Mom (Hedda), Dawn, Mitch, and Denise.

TABLE OF CONTENTS

Introduction: *We Can Do This Hard, or We Can Do This Easy* ix
Ultimately, It's All About Communication xi
You Know It Exists, But Do You Know Where It Is? xv

PART 1: THE DIFFICULT CONVERSATIONS 1
Death (or Terminal Illness) 5
Money 11
Driving 15
Hiring Help 21
Leaving Home 23

PART 2: CONVERSATION TIPS FOR COMMUNICATING WITH AGING ADULTS 29
Communicating with Aging Loved Ones 31
Ten Communication Absolutes 35
Communication with The General Public 37
Communicating with Doctors/Clinicians 39
Go Bag and Tool Kits for a Less Stressed Hospital Stay 43

PART 3: YOUR SUPPORT/CARE TEAM 45
Creating a Care Team 47
Co-Caregiving – Empowering Others to Assist 51
Friends and Neighbors 61
Finding Your People 61
Experts/Professionals to Add to the Care Team 63
Support Group 65

PART 4: COMMUNICATION IN THE TECHNOLOGY AGE 67
Communicating in the Technology Age 69
Video Etiquette 71
Dirty Dozen Video Conference Gathering Etiquette and Tips 73

PART 5: GENERAL CONVERSATION TIPS 77
Self-Care vs. The Gloom and Doom Reporters 79
Conversation Starters for Aging Loved Ones 81
Be the Protector 83

Acknowledgments 85
Fern Pessin Bio 87

INTRODUCTION
WE CAN DO THIS HARD, OR WE CAN DO THIS EASY

Getting through your day-to-day as an individual or parent of young children is often challenging enough without worrying about caring for others. As we navigate life's milestones, most of us will eventually arrive at the point where we begin to worry about our parents, partners, and grown children with their families. When you arrive at this milestone and feel like your accumulated wisdom might be helpful, you might find that offering what seems to you as logical decision-making comes under attack. You're perhaps being pushed away with comments like, "You're intruding," "It's none of your business," "Mind your own life and leave mine alone," or "I don't need your help because I'm fine."

The clues that someone you love needs guidance or assistance become more frequent, and what you brushed away as *nothing* earlier suddenly seems urgent, like the yellow caution or red warning lights are being activated in your subconscious. Someone you love will get hurt, possibly hurt another person, or lose their assets: life savings, home, business, etc. *How can I stand by and let that happen?* you wonder.

After a few incidents (or a close call), you will probably find yourself saying something like "When can we talk?" to your loved one because you feel in your heart that you can't be silent any longer. How you approach these types of conversations can lead to confrontation or collaboration. Wouldn't you rather have the latter?

Perhaps you have spoken with other people in the orbit of your loved one to ask if they're noticing the same things you see. You may ask them if they want to come together to present shared thoughts in an interventional manner. Be advised that this might appear to your loved one as confrontational—an all-of-you-against-me scenario.

Perhaps writing and coordinating a plan to fix the situation is a good option. Or maybe calling in people you know can take charge and fix a situation seems like a quick way to get things right again. Be advised that this might come across as you trying to be the boss, that you're helicopter parenting them, or that you believe they're incapable. No grown adult wants to feel that they're being reduced to a child or invalid status.

While someone still retains awareness about what's happening around them (at least some), your presentation style for jumping in to help a loved one can make or break your future relationship. As they say in action movies and crime dramas, "You can do this hard, or you can do this easy; which do you want?" Good cop/bad cop. With some finesse in your approach, you can create a collaborative relationship and get done what you know needs to happen to keep your loved one safe and healthy and preserve their assets.

I have gone down this bumpy road myself and have the bruises to prove it was rough. I ultimately came to understand that it was not *what* I said but *how* I said it that was the issue. I want to share what I learned to keep you from being bruised and battered. I've also included anecdotes shared with me by other caregivers because none of us are in this alone. One in five adults is caregiving right now, all around the world.

In the following chapters, I offer variations for people who learn and absorb in different ways or have different priorities to help guide you through this challenging time. Choose what works for you or use my suggestions to inspire your version.

ULTIMATELY, IT'S ALL ABOUT COMMUNICATION

Actual conversation with my mother:

"I'm tired. You watch your dad for a while. I'm going to take a half-hour nap in the bedroom."

To my retreating mother, I yelled, "Mom, stop! You can't take a nap now."

"I'm so tired," she whined like a four-year-old as she turned and faced me.

"I am on Zoom, Mom. I am not in the room with Dad!" I was panicking. I tried to rationalize with Mom. "You can't just walk away. He's sitting on a bar stool at the counter. He could fall off when he tries to get out of the chair, and I won't be able to help him. He's eating. What if he chokes? You can't just walk away, Mom!"

My mother gave me an Emmy-worthy performance of a teenage "you're so annoying" eye roll followed by a heavy sigh and, shoulders slumping forward, shuffled back to where Dad was staring at me on the computer screen in front of him, probably thinking he was watching a television show starring his daughter.

"He looks fine," my mom assessed, obviously thinking, *So why are you bothering me?*

"But Mom, I'm not in the room. You need to be with him. The aide just left an hour ago. Didn't you rest while she was there? Why are you so tired?"

"You just don't know how hard this is…." She choked up, and tears started to well in her eyes as she continued her pleas to let her nap. We compromised and agreed that she could sit in Dad's royal-blue Ultrasuede electric recliner in the same room, visible to the computer camera so I could see her and she could hear me.

The chair whirred as she reclined back, and with another theatrical heavy sigh, she closed her eyes. I resumed trying to connect with my father, who was well into dementia blankness.

I understood that my mother's fatigue was due to depression and exhaustion. Her husband for more than sixty years was disappearing, but a man was still present every day in the apartment and needed care. My father had Alzheimer's. He wore a diaper. We battled hallucinations with pharmaceuticals and won the day on that front as Dad was no longer tearing his hands apart trying to remove hair from his palms. He was no longer leaving his apartment to walk the corridor in the wee hours of the morning in his boxer shorts to silence people he heard talking in his head. But he still had no control over his bladder and would fall when he forgot to grab the walker. He needed reminders on how to eat and drink. He could not be left unsupervised.

When the aides came (every day, all day), Mom could leave the apartment to play with the friends she had made in her new adult community. She could enjoy a life free from day-to-day chores because I spent half a year persuading my father that living in an independent community would be the best choice for my mother in this very situation.

Back then, when I was in *influencing* mode, at various times, my mother accused me of butting in, trying to kick her out of her condo home, and trying to be the boss of her. In retrospect, she was delighted with the move because she had everything at her fingertips like a lady of leisure: a driver on call, personal trainer, trips planned for her, weekly entertainment, food prepared and served, an emergency team a pull-cord away, and people all around her who praised her as a hero for taking care of Dad. "You did good," my mother later said. While there was praise for the new lifestyle I brought her, it came with a but—always a but—and a list of everything wrong with the place. Do you know anyone like this who must always knock everything?

Meanwhile, on this day when Mom wanted nothing but a nap, my dad was snarling at my mother's retreating back because earlier, she had left him sitting on the toilet and wasn't there to help him when he was finished. He didn't know the words to express his anger. He was disappointed in her and embarrassed that he required this kind of help. My dad's hands flicked away my mother's ministrations like swatting an annoying fly, and the lack of a smile or ability to connect with me made his status quite clear to me, even over Zoom. I was on TV—not his daughter, not his friend. But it was COVID, and I couldn't be there.

Why did Mom leave Dad in this humiliating position on the toilet? She justified it by saying she had to log on and set up for our Zoom appointment. So, it was really (yet again) *all* my fault. The joys of caregiving.

Caregiver Burnout

Somehow, even though I was not in the room with them, I was also thoroughly exhausted. Trying to help them make decisions, maintain their health, and manage their expenses and logistics was time-consuming at minimum. I worried that Mom's own cognitive decline might worsen, to the point where she would no longer care for Dad. Or (statistically a 65 percent chance) Mom would have a health incident requiring someone to care for her while Dad was still alive.

I worried about having all the bases covered and asked questions persistently so I could manage everything with the knowledge of how my parents would want things to be managed/handled.

My greatest joy when my father passed away came from my dad's therapist (another thing I arranged despite his initial objection). She told me Dad always talked about how proud he was of me. He was confident I would take good care of Mom and him when he couldn't and was happy with all my decisions on their behalf. He loved me. What more could a daughter hope to hear?

Do you know how you would want people to care for you? Do they know what you want? Did you do the research and know the options for your loved one(s) in a variety of situations? If you have, bravo! Not many take the time in advance.

The challenge is always communication. How do we talk to our loved ones about this, especially if they have physical or cognitive deficits? How do we raise critical topics and decisions without meddling? How do we tell our siblings what we think would work for our parents without them thinking we are trying to be the hero or push them out of the picture? How do we talk to a declining spouse about the care best for them? How do we get the doctors on board with including us in the information-sharing journey? How do we communicate with strangers who misunderstand what they're seeing? When it is time to bring in extra help, how do we get our loved one to be okay with that?

When it comes to providing help in the form of asking someone to leave their home (as I did) to move to a place where there are people around to check in with them or to have aides come into the home, or to get a service dog that can sniff for a diabetes insulin crisis or ask someone to wear a fall monitor and so on…

How do we bring up these discussions without seeming like a bully, a know-it-all, an intruder? We know it will help; we want it done for our peace of mind. The intended does not want change. End of discussion. Now what?

The most despised conversation is when someone should no longer be driving. Talking about money is not easy either. So many secrets. And asking someone to let you help when they're so accustomed to being independent brings in all kinds of prejudices and emotional baggage packed and dragged throughout your relationship.

There's a way to have difficult conversations and make decisions without tears, door slamming, or yelling. We ideally want to avoid bruising egos or being abused for offering help. There are so many heated points to discuss.

This guidebook will take you through strategies for approaching any challenging topic or difficult conversation so you don't destroy all the good in your relationships.

A NOTE:

Assessing your loved one's physical, emotional, and cognitive status as early in the game as possible will provide you with a sense of what lies ahead so you can make your to-do list and design a road map to plan for all contingencies. To not overwhelm people with tons of info here, I suggest the assessment worksheets in my book, *I'll Be Right There: A Guidebook for Adults Caring for Their Aging Parents*. And, I have answered common questions in blogs on my website at www.illberightthere.com.

I'm Not Gonna Live Forever You Know: A Personal Archive for Sharing Your Wishes with Your Loved Ones provides a place to put all the information anyone will need to manage affairs and offer help in various situations. The questions in both books will help you set up a plan for short and long-term care.

YOU KNOW IT EXISTS, BUT DO YOU KNOW WHERE IT IS?

I aim to help guide you through some uncomfortable (and possibly awkward) conversations you may need to have with your parents, partner, or designated representative "in case." You'll know when it's time for these talks.

My friend Amy and I were discussing the challenges of communication within families. She and her husband, both in their forties, had completed all their legal documents "in case something should happen to both of us at the same time." She also had a collection of paperwork from her parents.

When I was thirteen, my parents went on their first international trip. They took separate flights to ensure that if one plane went down, one parent would still return to care for their children. Is that extreme? Maybe. Maybe not. That kind of consideration influences the lens through which I see the world. Amy was of a similar mind.

Before traveling out of town, Amy had left all her essential information in a sealed envelope with her siblings.

Amy had shared her family's preparations with her in-laws but got the sense that they believed if they began to speak about preparing for death or incapacity, death would soon be upon them. Amy could not believe that her husband's family was so afraid to share *any* information about their estate, home, and paperwork with their children.

Since I've been caregiving and attending support groups, I have heard too many horror stories about what happens to people's assets and lives when they have no one who knows how to help. Amy and I share the belief that being prepared is better than not.

I don't think my parents were surprised when I brought up their possible incapacity early on and what would happen to them if I was incapacitated as their eldest daughter. It wasn't comfortable. It's not a cheery topic. But maybe since my dad was in the business of doing people's taxes and hearing about intimate family money issues, and I worked in the office with him for eight years, we tended toward sharing and discussion, knowing the consequences when you don't.

What happens if we're intubated in the age of pandemics, wildfires, and hurricanes? What happens if you lose your memory or ability to speak due to illness or accident? So many things could happen just going through a regular day. I read about a famous athlete out riding his bicycle when a driver misjudged the distance between his car and the cyclist, sending the cyclist flying. The athlete wound up in critical care, unconscious, and ultimately confined for life to a wheelchair.

My friend spent eleven years caring for her parents. Two years after losing her mother, no longer having caregiving responsibilities, she was hospitalized. She had a stroke, and testing revealed a Stage 4 glioblastoma. Fatal. Six months to live. Unable to process thoughts and communicate following the stroke, her family delayed treatment decisions because they didn't know what she wanted. She had told her friends but didn't leave specifics in writing for her family (her designated representatives) what to do if she was mentally incapacitated. As friends, we could not do anything but hold her hand. It's not enough to have created the papers; someone you trust must know where they are.

I don't want to scramble to locate someone else's documents and data during a crisis without a clue on where to start. If I'm tearing the house apart, searching for a health document the hospital needs only to find out it had been relocated to a safe deposit box in a bank, it would be helpful to have that information before I waste hours searching.

I told Amy to look at this fear as I prepare for inclement weather. When you carry an umbrella "just in case," it hardly ever rains; if it does rain, you stay dry. You keep a hurricane preparedness/power outage kit in the house in the Florida, Texas, and Louisiana areas. You keep an evacuation or go bag when you live in places with flash floods, tornadoes, or wildfires. You prepare for blizzards and mass snow fall when you live in Vermont or Colorado. So why wouldn't you prepare for an unexpected, uncontrollable change in health and wellness to make things easier for your family—"just in case"?

Clear communication with your family is essential to creating and maintaining harmony. Sharing information and working cooperatively with your siblings will reduce the chance of confusion, fighting, and indecision in critical, possibly urgent situations if something should happen to your parents. Sharing your wishes with a spouse, loved one, sibling, or professional is the only way to ensure that your wishes are followed when you can no longer communicate.

We don't expect any of these things to happen. But with planning, if the situation arises, we will be less stressed, and it's good to know someone has your back, especially for people who live alone at any age.

This guidebook includes tips on communicating directly with loved ones and aging people. You'll learn how to help communicate your loved one's intentions to physicians and other medical staff and bring awareness to the public when you're out and about to avoid embarrassment. I offer conversation starters on significant issues such as no longer driving, arrangements for the end of life, financial and medical decisions, bringing in help, or moving out of the home.

We'll explore how you can bring up your wishes and requests with people asking to support you when you cannot care for yourself. Hopefully, you'll be able to talk more easily with your children about your preferences related to various issues that may arise as you age.

These heavy conversations typically bring on high levels of anxiety. This guidebook is designed to relieve some pressure and provide tools to make this communication process less stressful.

PART 1
THE DIFFICULT CONVERSATIONS

Death
Money
Driving
Hiring Help
Moving

When the Time Comes to Have the Difficult Conversations

Most want to live with dignity, age well, and live longer, stronger, and safer at home. Of course. But things happen; bodies age, and situations change. If conversations are delayed for too long, the information a designated caregiver needs to have may become impossible to find. It doesn't have to be that way. However, to make it easier later, you must break down the barriers and get through the awkward and difficult conversations early on.

Conversations must occur between parents and their children (or vice versa), spouse-to-spouse, and potentially among siblings. The person who will care for you needs to know your wishes. If you are the designated care partner for someone, you will want to initiate these conversations.

I Am Just Not Ready for This

Procrastinating on discussing serious topics (death, money, driving, moving, health) is common. You are not alone if you find yourself delaying. These topics may feel taboo. Or the number of things you need to know seems overwhelming. Sometimes, you'd prefer to avoid information that is intimate/personal.

If you live far away from the person you provide care for, you might not be able to be in the same room to collect the answers and information you need. And while face-to-face is always preferred, technology exists to make this less of an issue now.

Whatever the reason, whether you don't want to or can't be there yourself, you might consider engaging emotionally unattached, outside facilitators to help you get the ball rolling.

Impartial Stranger – If your relationship with your loved one is such that they won't listen to you (just like we didn't believe anything our parents said when we were teenagers, remember that?), consider enlisting the help of a respected advisor, trusted neighbor, or willing proxy to have these conversations for you. Sometimes, the outsider will have better luck getting answers.

Respected Leader – Engaging someone in a position of authority who is admired locally is another way to gather answers: perhaps a professional with specific expertise (lawyer, doctor, financial advisor/accountant), a clergy person, or religious leader (they have the ear of the Lord, right?) or a counselor/therapist (so, how do you feel about that?). The leader of a nonprofit organization who helps people in your situation or someone who regularly practices advising from a strong impartial or diplomatic perspective (a writer, judge, teacher, military official, or police officer) could also prove helpful.

Mediator – Maybe you've started the conversation, but your family cannot agree, or you are dealing with a head-in-the-sand personality. You might try a professional mediator to facilitate answers to guided questions and to construct an action plan. You can ask your estate lawyer if their office handles this or if they can provide a list of licensed mediators in the area. Do a web search using the zip code to find local providers. If your person is elderly, there are specifically trained and certified elder care mediators to help you through. Your Area Agency on Aging should be able to provide suitable contact information, local price ranges, and more education about what to expect.

Caseworker – When trust cannot be established, or personalities clash due to issues from the past, when end goals are out of sync with all parties involved, a paid caseworker can be hired to facilitate and offer suggestions that are in the incapacitated person's best interest. This kind of support is essential when decisions about health care, legal, or financial issues cannot be promptly agreed upon (and no one is designated decision-maker).

Death Doula – At some point, when we face the thought of dying, we may feel it is a very private issue, and we want someone who will be there to guide us through. A family may not be comfortable discussing end wishes with their loved one. A death doula is a support person who may or may not have medical training and will provide emotional assistance to a dying individual before and during death. A death doula is also there to guide the family and caregivers calmly and peacefully through the process. (You can find a death doula by web searching or asking a local hospice organization.)

The end goal is to follow the wishes of your loved one/care partner. You can help a facilitator gather the necessary information by providing a list of items, information, and decisions you believe are needed. Read on to get some ideas for what to add to your list.

Whether you do this yourself or bring in an outsider to help—bite the bullet, as they say—try some of the following gentler (No, Mom, I'm not trying to steal your money!) options for opening discussions.

DEATH (OR TERMINAL ILLNESS)

The forbidden topic. The great equalizer. Mortality. If we don't discuss it, death won't happen, right? Of course not. So, let's get this big one out of the way first.

In America, talking about death is forever being put on the do-tomorrow list. What about death positivity? What about the idea that speaking about our death with our family and sharing our wishes with our loved ones or designated care partners brings about less fear, reduces taboos, and allows us to focus on the joy of living? The knowledge of handling everything so your family does not have to fret over having done something wrong or against your wishes is very calming for the living.

In other cultures, death is celebrated in the remembrance of life well lived. The Hispanic culture has Día de los Muertos, where families gather to share stories and eat food loved by the departed. In South Korea, they have Chuseok, a harvest festival commemorating ancestral spirits. Families visit the graves of their ancestors to clean the sites, make offerings of food, and perform rituals as a sign of respect and remembrance. Why not create a conversation now with the people you will help or those who will help you when passing?

You're reading this book or talking to family/friends/advisors and recognize that steps must be taken, but bringing up death seems invasive. You may have questions like:

- Will my loved one believe I want them to die?
- Will my parents think I'm after their assets?
- Will they think I am looking out for what's in it for me?
- Will my siblings be offended if I raise this as a discussion we need to have?
- My neighbor relies on me for everything, but will he be put off if I raise the topic of his eventual death?

What's your reason for avoiding this topic? Open your mind, channel your inner Cher in *Moonstruck*, and "Snap out of it!"

Terminal Illness

Suppose your loved one can understand a diagnosis of a terminal illness and all the complications and changes that will occur between diagnosis and passing. In that case, your role is to be supportive and compassionate.

Suppose your loved one cannot understand because of clinical or emotional incapacity. In that case, your role is even more important as all the decisions for health, legal, and financial issues must also be managed. Naturally, compassion should still be offered.

One's first reaction to hearing an undesirable diagnosis is to shut down, and everything that came after the diagnosis news will likely be forgotten. A blank mind will be all that will be recalled after that meeting. At diagnosis, the caregiver's role is to help someone come to grips with the news and determine a plan of action and what kind of team needs to be put in place—but maybe not immediately. Research may be needed to get the information to find out what the doctor said. Ask about support from a nurse navigator at the hospital or doctor's office to help with this. You may need to get the HIPAA form signed by the patient so the doctor can release the information for you to provide support.

Your communication style will depend on how the individual is handling the news. You may need to be patient until things sink in before beginning logistics discussions. You may need to take a step back, or you might need to be there to hold a hand, lend a shoulder, or give a hug. Some people appreciate a joke or a lighthearted approach to discussing a heavy topic. Others prefer a more clinical approach with details and data. Still, others would rather not know anything and have you handle it all. No book will give you an answer that works for everyone.

Some questions you can ask yourself to guide your communication style and approach include:

- ❖ Do symptoms and outcomes need to be explained again?
- ❖ Are there experts who can be brought in or materials available to help my loved one process the information until they fully comprehend and can decide the course of treatment?
- ❖ Your efforts to help someone line up resources should include a discussion about how much involvement from you they want.

If your loved one is angry, belligerent, or in denial, read the coming chapters to find tips on how to communicate that may work for you.

Once a diagnosis is made, knowing if someone wants to fight for their life or receive palliative care (keep them free of pain) and let them stop fighting will influence everything in the future. That is the conversation that needs to happen after the prognosis is understood.

The most important thing, in my opinion, is to find out the end goal for the patient. The Five Wishes document is explained further in this section, which helps answer these questions before anything occurs.

Is the quality of life for the remaining time the most crucial factor to your loved one, or is it time to be spent fighting for a longer life? Is that acceptable if treatment makes the remaining time after a terminal diagnosis miserable? Or can you help someone enjoy every moment without pain and suffering—having love and experiences to treasure instead of being bedbound or having headaches and bowel issues, too sick to engage with loved ones? This is a time to consider the patient's wishes and not think about what you want or how much you want to hang on to your loved one. This is challenging. I know.

If you don't agree with their decision to either fight or go, and you hold your ground, you might lose your loved one's faith in you as a caregiver. How you broach this topic is delicate. Sharing your opinion in a nonconfrontational manner is imperative. The conversation should always lead with wanting to be supportive. Expressing how you feel is okay as long as how you feel is not the criteria for moving forward. Honoring the wishes of your sick loved one is the priority.

End of Life

The talk must happen. No... not birds and bees this time. One unplanned health incident, and you're in trouble. No one wakes up and says, "Hmmm. I think I will have a stroke today. Let me get my affairs in order so my family will know what I want." So, pull yourself together and begin this conversation. You'll be much less stressed once everything is all processed and in your files.

"How?" you want to know. How do you bring this up? Many people feel that bringing up death or end-of-life plans will be confrontational, aggressive, or combative because it's so emotional. It speaks to our core survival instincts. Maybe even our superstitious side: You will bring it if you say it.

Here are some possible gentle conversation openers that are loving and should help ease your family into the dreaded discussions—before anyone is in grieving mode:

- ❖ "I love you and hope you live forever, but I'm pretty sure that's not likely. I want to understand what you'd like me to do for your final plans."
- ❖ "Mom/Dad, the family is meeting to discuss our wishes for care in crisis, emergency, or death. We're meeting (insert day, time, location). Will you participate?"
- ❖ "My friend's father (or... I read that someone's father) recently passed away, and the poor guy didn't have a clue as to what his father wanted and what had already been taken care of. He spent $13,000 on a burial and funeral and then, a few months later, found papers while cleaning out his father's home, saying that his father had prepaid to be cremated. Can we talk about what you'd like so I don't do the wrong thing?"
- ❖ Pull out a Five Wishes document (explained in detail at https://fivewishes.org on the Aging with Dignity organization website) and ask your loved one if they will fill one out with you. Explain that you want them to know your wishes, and you'd like to know theirs. Inviting your friends, parents, and siblings to participate and complete their Five Wishes reduces any feelings of being confrontational as your request for information is no longer directed to only one person.

The Five Wishes will guide you through questions like:

- o If you are diagnosed with a terminal illness, living in pain, or unable to care for yourself, what would you like us/your family to do?
- o Can we talk about hospice care? How do you feel about end-of-life caregiving? What is your preference for palliative (living without pain) care? Do you prefer to be at home, the hospital, or a residential facility?
- o When you're not feeling well, do you want to be left to yourself or prefer company more often than not?
- o Are you an organ donor?
- o What can I bring to keep you comfortable if you're not well? Music? Your pet? A certain scent? A picture to look at? Visitors? Your bathrobe or shawl?

And so on.

My father made it clear he wanted to be at home. My mother said she preferred to be in a hospital setting. Dad said, quite seriously, that I should put a pillow over his face before putting him in a nursing home. He died two weeks after going to skilled nursing when he developed COVID. We knew that he knew we had honored his wishes and kept him home as long as possible.

Once the conversation has begun, you might want to discuss the elements that can be preplanned and prepaid. "Can we talk about your funeral? Do you know what you would like? Have you thought about…?"

- Would you like to be buried or cremated?
- Where would you like to be buried?
- Who would you like at your funeral/memorial service?
- Do you have cremation urns/casket selected?
- Where would you like your ashes scattered?
- Have you prepaid for a funeral or burial?
- Do you have funeral insurance?
- Did you talk to the VA about free burial in a Veterans' cemetery?
- What do you want on your gravestone?
- What kind of service would you prefer?
- Do you have a list of people you'd like us to notify when you pass?
- Do you want to donate your brain or body to science?
- Do you have preferences for your obituary, headstone, and epitaphs?

While your loved ones still can, asking them to write or help you write an obituary, what they want printed on their headstone, and any epitaphs might be helpful. What pictures do they want you to use?

If there are specific things your loved ones want to be said about them or messages they want you to give to people attending a funeral, wake, or memorial/celebration service on their behalf, ask them to write the messages down so you can include them in the services.

Completing these tasks will give you all a sense of control and comfort—one less thing for the to-do list.

Joe and Sarah

I met my mother's neighbors, Joe and Sarah, in the dining room of their independent living community. I spent many convivial meals with the lovely couple in their 90s. Sara always mentioned how impressed she was with all the advice and support I gave my parents. They occasionally asked me for advice, which I readily provided. The one thing I kept impressing on them was the need to talk to their family about their wishes. They kept putting it off. I talked to their daughter, and she put it off. For two years, they didn't think it was important enough to prioritize. They were in their 90s, just when did they think would be the right time?

Joe dropped out of conversations at the dinner table due to hearing loss. Eventually, over a year, he and my father just sat at the table and ate while their wives chatted. Ultimately, Joe became unmanageable physically as neither his bones nor muscles could hold him upright; he was a rag doll. Sarah refused to hire an aide because she didn't want strangers in their apartment. She wouldn't bring in hospice, though it was clear Joe wasn't well. All this happened while Sarah progressively lost her vision and hearing and thus became more fragile. Sarah needed guidance and resources that hospice or the VA would have provided, free of charge. But she was stubborn and refused to admit she needed help.

One night, Joe needed help getting to the bathroom. Sarah wrenched her back trying to get him up when he fell instead of taking our advice to call for a lift assist from the local firehouse. Joe was eventually taken to the hospital; unfortunately, he passed away after being dropped by an aide there. Sarah moaned that it was "so sudden" and fretted that she didn't know what to do. The hospital wanted to know who was coming to get the body. Sarah had no clue—and no help. She decided to call her granddaughter, who then jumped in, researched, and found a funeral home. From there, it was a scramble to get the funeral approved at the veteran's cemetery and pull together a list of people to invite and their contact information. They had to start assembling the photos and eulogy materials while deep in mourning.

I have such heartache for this family. Some advance discussions about who to call when one of them passed away and what they would want would have made life much easier. Asking the granddaughter to be the surrogate planner for this would have made the next steps at Joe's death less overwhelming, and she would have been prepared. As it was, Sarah compared her panicked situation to our calm situation when my dad passed away and wondered why there was such a difference.

When my dad passed away a few months before Joe, I already had the funeral home arrangements made. When the hospice worker called to notify me of Dad's passing, I had the funeral home's twenty-four-hour number handy, and I was done. A few hours later, I checked with the funeral home, and they had already retrieved the body, called the Brain Bank (where Dad was pre-registered), had the brain harvested, and the body was heading to the crematorium later that day. The ashes would all be returned to me along with Dad's relatively new pacemaker (so it could be donated for reuse in a country where they allow recycled medical equipment). I was sad but completely calm. I already had a video collage of ninety photos ready. I already had spoken to Mom's building management to see if we could host the Celebration of Life service there. I had already discussed a service with our clergyman and provided him with notes in case none of our family was in the right frame of mind to speak. I went down the checklist of things to do and called or emailed Dad's final details. There were no new decisions to make. This was everything Dad and Mom wanted and what we had discussed over two years, step by step, and it was quickly implemented.

In moments of crisis, when we are in emotional distress, it is counterproductive to suddenly need to make huge decisions that will impact us financially, emotionally, and possibly physically when advanced planning and open conversations negate the tension and panic of last-minute scrambling.

MONEY

Whoa! Another touchy topic! Ben Franklin said nothing can be certain except death and taxes, right? So, let's get this topic out of the way next.

First, my mother's ninety-two-year-old friend Gloria recently told me, "Make sure you tell people that they need to know about the expenses for day-to-day living. Having a spouse take care of everything is lovely, except when that spouse passes or has dementia, and you don't know how much electricity costs, you are at a severe disadvantage!" So, cautionary word, make sure your loved ones understand their expenses and budget, and perhaps they will be so kind as to share it with you so you can help if they start forgetting to pay those bills.

Most of the time, your parents or other loved ones probably don't feel the need for you to be all up in their personal financial business. Unless they've been getting money from you to help support them, they most likely believe their money is theirs, and you should keep your hands off it.

Maybe someone doesn't want the family to know they are more or less wealthy than the family believes. Or maybe someone has property or valuables that, once shared, may be the source of conflict over who gets what. There are personal reasons to keep things private. But what happens when one spouse suddenly becomes ill, and the bills need to be paid, and the other spouse doesn't know how to balance a checkbook or access and use online accounts? What happens when the expenses for day-to-day living suddenly increase with nursing care or hospital expenses? Who will help then? What if there's a fire or flood, earthquake, tornado, or hurricane, and all the paperwork in the house is gone? Running around during an emergency or time-pressured situation to figure this all out is a sure stressor and is unnecessary if you help your loved one plan. Surely you don't want to pay all these bills and expenses yourself if the resources are available from the person incurring the expenses? But do you have access? Do you have details?

While a person is still alive, getting legal access to their funds or accounts is near impossible. First, you must know where the accounts are, plus account numbers, balances, and passwords. Then, a time-consuming declaration of incapacity must be filed (which may require a lawyer and doctor); meanwhile, things begin falling through the cracks. Having a Durable Power of Attorney (naming the person with permitted access to financial and health information) for your loved one will make keeping the household and finances running smoothly much easier.

Money Makes the World Go 'Round

The conversations about money don't have to be about specific amounts. Still, they should ensure you can assist and get what is needed when and if necessary, without being bogged down going through legal hoops or trying to figure out what to locate.

During these preliminary dialogues, avoid discussing an inheritance, possible investments to consider, or the fact that your loved one could become dependent on you if things go awry. These are sure ways to put people on the defensive.

Nonthreatening conversation starters might include:

- ❖ "A friend just had to get money out of her own bank account to pay her mother's bills because her mom was in rehab after an accident. The bank wouldn't let my friend anywhere near her mom's account. My friend doesn't have a lot of her own money. Her mom could lose the condo if the Homeowners' Association dues and taxes aren't paid. I don't want that to happen to you. Can we work on having me as your backup in case of an emergency?"

Connect the potential issue with relatable examples. Maybe you can find information on neighbors or friends who had a difficult time with finances and suggest that you'd like to be there to help so things never go that way for your loved one. Reassure all parties that you want to guarantee your loved ones have the resources to get everything they need and want and retain their money for them as long as possible. You'd like to assist them in finding the right local help to be sure that happens. You're happy to be as involved as they want you to be. The more you know, the more you can help.

To demonstrate that you are not after their money but are concerned about health service delivery, try this approach:

- ❖ "I don't need to know the actual numbers for your assets, but if something happens to you, I will need to know where to look to manage your affairs. Could you put all the information in a sealed envelope, leave it with a lawyer or friend, and let me know where and who has it so I can get it and handle things for you if something happens? If you could include a Durable Power of Attorney and Health Care Advance Directive giving me the authority to handle your financial matters upon your incapacity, that would speed things along when and if needed." (Whoever is named as the Executor of a Will will only care for things after someone dies.)

Hand them some research you've done. "Here are some articles about managing your finances into retirement."

- ❖ "If you don't want me involved, I understand, but maybe you could find a reputable financial consultant to set things up for you. Perhaps you could work with a local financial concierge or personal assistant who will have access to your accounts in case you can't handle something personally. Maybe you'll be traveling on a world cruise or having a medical procedure and need someone else to handle things. A financial concierge can help you pay your bills, manage invoices and charitable giving, ensure you don't get scammed, and so on. It doesn't have to be me, but I want to confirm someone will be watching out for you."

❖ "I have been hearing so many stories on the news about scams. It would be best if you weren't conned. You've worked so hard to create a nest egg. Can we discuss your strategies? Will you agree to tell me about any new things you're looking into so I can check whether it's a fraud?"

Once you get your loved one opening up a bit or at least get their money handled by a trustworthy, qualified expert with experience, you can be more at ease.

If you don't already have your own financial and legal documents completed, you'll want to go through the list of what you have on hand and determine what you still want to collect. I was diagnosed with eye cancer at sixty-two years old and needed radiation and surgeries. I was happy to know I had already sent information about where to find everything in my apartment to my sister. I left a spare key with a neighbor and a lock box down the hall. I could focus on myself and know everything would be handled.

Sample List of Documents

- ☐ Deeds/Ownership Documents for Properties
- ☐ Last Will & Testament
- ☐ Power of Attorney
- ☐ Durable Power of Attorney or Healthcare Power of Attorney/Proxy
- ☐ Beneficiaries List
- ☐ Living Will/Advanced Healthcare Directive
- ☐ Five Wishes Document
- ☐ Funeral Paperwork (Policy/Prepaid Info)
- ☐ Revocable or Irrevocable Trust
- ☐ Back Tax Returns (5 to 7 Years)
- ☐ IRA/401(K)/503B Account Details
- ☐ All Bank Accounts
- ☐ Debit Cards
- ☐ Credit Cards
- ☐ Monthly Auto-Pay Accounts
- ☐ Real Estate and Property Taxes
- ☐ Mortgage
- ☐ Community Common Charges
- ☐ Monthly Bills
- ☐ Medication List
- ☐ Medical History
- ☐ Insurance Cards and Plan information (Life, Medical, Long-Term Care, Auto, Liability, etc.)
- ☐ Donor Information
- ☐ DNR/DNI or Health Care Directives

DRIVING

The first sign of losing independence is when the car keys are taken away—and that feels good to no one. Having the conversation about turning over the keys to the car is one of the toughest caregiving responsibilities. The right to drive is one of the most fervently defended.

Of course, like with health, money, and moving, you can avoid this conversation indefinitely. On the one hand, perhaps you dread becoming the person your loved one calls to drive them everywhere to do anything. The longer they drive, the less of a burden they are on you. On the other hand, if they get into an accident and harm themselves, you're possibly caring for someone with debilitating physical issues. Or if they hurt someone else, you're now dealing with emotional trauma accompanied by a possible lawsuit, car repair expenses, or even jail time. So maybe this conversation is something worth taking time to prepare for? There are multiple considerations:

- ❖ The car itself—whose car is it? Ownership, storage, and maintenance of a vehicle.
- ❖ Cognitive or physical ability to drive a car at all.

STOP! In the Name of Love

Why should someone stop driving if nothing has happened? Yet. Our wise elder lawyer said, "It never happens until it does." That sticks with me. It only takes one time before something becomes a life-changing event. The direct approach, "You need to stop driving before you kill yourself or someone else," only works in rare cases when someone has already self-determined that they might be ready to stop driving. If you don't want to be excommunicated, here are some more gentle messages that can help ease someone away from the wheel—when delivered with patience and love.

One other note is to keep in mind that this takes time. Slowly (over a few months) introduce these ideas until you reach the best result. Only in a critical situation can you justify removing keys without discussion.

Cost of Ownership

If the car is used for trips to the grocery store each week or to restaurants occasionally, and that's pretty much it, you might want to bring up that the cost of car ownership may be a reason to stop driving: "Think of the money you can save!"

Adding a comparison of auto-related expenses versus as-needed services will help if they are not tied emotionally to the benefits of the car. Please recognize that for some, going out to run errands or, in my grandmother's case, 4:00 p.m. early-bird dinners at a restaurant, are the only reasons to get out of the house. Loneliness is a significant factor in hanging on to the keys.

Try comparing auto ownership to using a ride-sharing app (Lyft or Uber are the current most common) or local taxis (they now take online booking in many places) or community transportation (bus, train, senior/disabled low or no-cost buses, community vans/drivers). Suggest offering a neighbor a few bucks for a ride so your loved one will have company, too.

Having things delivered to the home is easy now—from groceries to pharmacy items to household supplies and furniture. The post office delivers stamps and mailing envelopes to the home, with regular mail delivery.

Senior and community centers offer group excursions for shopping at outlet malls and trips to entertainment, casinos, and nature parks.

Try to demonstrate to your loved one that they will still have everything they need and enjoy, even without a car. After all, you are not trying to keep them locked at home.

Distracted Driving Dangers

Anyone can be a great driver on an empty road or in a big open parking lot. It's dealing with other distracted drivers who may be anxiously texting about a work issue, trying to find directions, putting on makeup, shaving, trimming nose hairs, talking on the phone, changing music stations, or dealing with children or pets that cause the problems. "It's not you; it's them we're worried about!" is what we aim for here.

Unexpected Diversions

A few days ago, a couch fell off the pickup truck in front of me on the highway—at night! Can your loved one handle something like that? Other potential trouble spots: detours and road changes preventing your loved one from finding their familiar way to and from where they want to be. What about construction? Snow, rain, potholes, and detours? Driving requires concentrating on the road as well as being aware of the actions of the cars in front of, behind, and on either side of you. You must also be looking out for people walking into your path, cyclists on the road, and weaving cars around you, which can all cause accidents.

Physical Limitations

Can your loved one physically twist their body or head around to look out the rear windshield and both side windows before backing out of a parking space in the mall or grocery store parking lot? Or are they relying on backup and side camera technology for warnings?

Let's face it: Reaction time decreases with age and some progressive illnesses. Balance becomes affected. The ability to multitask decreases with age. Can you have that conversation with your loved one? Or is an outside person the best one to bring this discussion?

"I'm DONE!"

In my case, the decision about the car and whether my parents would keep a car was decided for us when my dad totaled his car on his final drive from New York to Florida. The first step—removing the car—was resolved.

I got away lucky because the second step, the idea of taking away the keys and agreeing not to drive at all, was made by my father. He didn't want to get behind the wheel of a car again after the accident. Although he emphasized that he was *able* to drive, he was *choosing* not to drive anymore. He was scared about getting into another accident and admitted to me that he didn't know how to get home or to familiar places anymore without someone directing him from the passenger seat. He shared a recent experience while in New York, where he spent three hours trying to get home from a store that was ten minutes away.

Helping your loved one stop driving, rather than mandating it, will help your relationship in the long run. Resentment is not fun! (That should be a bumper sticker.)

In the process of talking to my mother about not driving, the conversations started easy and appeared frequently, and over time, when I could see that her choosing to stop was not forthcoming, the worries and concerns I shared became more dramatic and scarier. Eventually, my mom chose to stop driving. Some of the concerns I put forth that helped her make that decision included (starting with the least offensive and building to the most provocative):

- ❖ "Just because you can turn the engine on, put your foot on the pedal to make the car go, put your foot on the brake to make the car stop, and turn the car off doesn't mean that you can be attentive to all the other things happening around you while driving." (I shared with her how she didn't hear or see an ambulance coming when we were shopping. I knew this because she asked why I wasn't going forward when the light turned green.)
- ❖ "You may be very focused on where you're going and what's ahead of you, but a good driver must also be aware of someone coming between two cars to cross the road in front of you unexpectedly."
- ❖ "It might not be you doing something wrong, but what if someone else is on the phone or texting and does something stupid, and you wind up in an accident because your reflexes have slowed down? You could be injured!"
- ❖ "What if you back into someone in a parking lot and injure them? Could you live with that?" (I reminded her of the stories she told us about having people slap the back of her car while she was backing out.)
- ❖ "What if you hit someone and wind up in jail? Can you imagine the rest of your life in jail?"
- ❖ "What if you injure or kill a dog, a cat, or a child? Could you live with that?"
- ❖ "What if you hit someone and the family sues you? Are you prepared to live without money? Bankruptcy?"
- ❖ "Dad is worried about you out there driving on your own. He panics when he doesn't know that you are safe." (This was the one that clinched it for Mom.)

Talking Didn't Work – What Now?

If the initial discussions (which will happen over time) don't work, more outside influencers may need to be employed.

Tracking Device

You might use a tracking device to record your loved one's driving activities. Where is the car going? How often? Unusual braking or jerky acceleration? Too slow? Too fast? Use the data to reassure yourself that things are okay or to discuss what you see with your loved one. (This device can also help locate your loved one if they wind up lost.) You can find these devices online and at auto supply stores. They can be hidden in the car if need be.

Tracking App

I used an app provided to me by AAA (Automobile Association of America) with my membership. It tracked my driving and gave me bonuses and reduced auto insurance fees, by keeping a good driving record. It tracks distractions, distance, time of day, speed, quality of driving, and more. Knowing you're being monitored makes you more attentive, like having a fitness tracker. You can offer this to your loved one to save money. But you should sign up for weekly reports to keep awareness of your loved one's driving skill status.

Driving Assessment

If you're being told you're too sensitive and overreacting, ask your loved one to go for a driving assessment. "How about we let a professional tell us if you still qualify to drive?" Check the internet for driving assessment services in your area. The Department of Motor Vehicles or local memory centers will likely have lists of providers.

Outside Influencers

If your loved one still won't give up the keys and you're sure that your loved one is a danger to themselves and others on the road, you can ask a doctor (people respect their doctors) to advise against driving. Could your lawyer go through the risks of tickets and accidents with your loved one? Can you ask the mechanic or another car expert to discuss what could happen with poor driving?

Motor Vehicle Department

If nothing you've tried has worked, the most dramatic route is to anonymously report your loved one to the DMV. Or you can provide a note from the doctor or the report from the driving assessment and ask them on the record to investigate the situation. The DMV will likely call your loved one in for a driving test or vision exam and may take away their license. This one is pretty emotional. There could be a backlash of anger or resentment headed your way. But isn't it better to be emotional now than to deal with all the possible consequences of an accident in the future?

With all of this, no matter what you do, remember to offer the options for remaining independent that I mentioned earlier.

My Mother's Driving Story

Why did mom need a car if I was taking my parents to all their medical appointments, out to dinners, and dropping Mom off and picking her up from volunteer duty? I wondered, what was she doing with the car? A hidden tracking device revealed that my mom was shopping. And then returning the things she bought. She stopped for fast food my father didn't want in the house. That's what she mostly did with the car.

Mom agreed to go through a driving assessment at the Green Memory Center in South Florida, confident she would pass with flying colors. After the driving test, the written exam, and the cognitive function assessment, the recommendation was that Mom was not to drive. If she chose to continue to drive, she should only go with someone else in the car, not go more than ten minutes from home, stay off the highways, and not drive at night.

How did Mom take this? She said happily, "I passed!"

"What?" I asked, confused. "It says here you shouldn't drive."

She corrected me, "It says I am not *recommended* to drive. It doesn't say I *shouldn't* drive." She had clearly taken a sip of her denial and narcissism cocktail; my mother saw what she wanted to see.

I admit I deliberately made it harder for Mom since she was so stubborn. I moved four miles away and took our shared car with me. (Am I horrible?) Mom would have to take a taxi to my home if she needed the car, so it was easier for me to pick her up and take her where she wanted to be. I was her chauffeur. (That's not too bad for her.) And then, I taught her how to use the Uber app. And we got her a permit for a local ride service for disabled people and seniors, which she could call twenty-four hours in advance. The senior center had a van that picked her up so she could still do volunteer work. Mom loved making new friends with the drivers of all these services.

When she moved to her senior living community with my dad, drivers and vans were part of the package and included in the rent. Within ten miles of the community, they would take her where she wanted to go. She had a friend in her community who drove to the same weekly caregiver support group, and they stopped at Target, Walmart, or Costco on the way home. Added to the Palm Tran service, which would take her anywhere in the county for $3.50, and her Uber app, Mom was all set and didn't need me, nor did she need to drive after all. She didn't lose her independence, although she missed the idea that she could go anywhere, any time by having a car in the parking lot. Freedom. She missed feeling that. But she stayed safe and that was peace-of-mind for my whole family.

HIRING HELP

"You are not chasing me out of my home!" Have you heard this when you even mentioned the idea of someone moving out? You recognize your loved one is starting to show signs of needing care or monitoring. The home is no longer safe, and you worry about falls, fires (electric or stove or oven), punctures (knives, furniture, tools, utensils), health crisis (heart attack, stroke, seizures), or any of a dozen other things. The point is...you worry.

You might be too far away to commute and help. You might not have a home conducive to inviting your loved one to live with you—whether it's got too many people, lots of stairs, is unsafe for someone with physical or mental challenges, or is just not an ideal emotional option. You might not have other people to rely on to step up, and you already have too much on your plate physically, financially, or emotionally. So, what to do?

One option is to bring in hired help. Broaching that idea is a conversation that often results in verbal fisticuffs. Ego and wanting to maintain independence are powerful core instincts. *How* you say things is as important as *what* you say.

You can avoid the hostility by following some simple guidelines:

- ❖ Please recognize that this person has needs they may not have shared with you.
- ❖ Recognize that home is more than just a physical space. There is a connection to the items in the home and the surrounding people, proximity to friends, and the views.
- ❖ Home is where everything is comfortable and familiar. If someone is losing memory, taking them away from home can push them into more significant memory loss. If they're losing sight or hearing, everything in the home is recognizable and thus easier to navigate.
- ❖ Home represents a routine that makes it feel like everything is going well. Change routine and the gaps in mental capacity become more evident and can lead to withdrawal, depression, and isolating behavior.

In general, any presentation on this topic should be prefaced with sharing how you care so much and are looking out for the best interest of your loved one, and this change would help you feel at peace knowing that your loved one is safe.

Like in the driving section, sharing your fear and being honest should reduce the anxiety of your loved one. You are not trying to be the boss; you are trying to alleviate a potential crisis.

Aim to come to a mutual understanding that your loved one needs to be safe and you'd like their input on the next steps.

You can begin by suggesting installing a camera (or several) for you to keep an eye on them long distance. You can discuss if the sound stays on or off. Do you *want* to hear everything? If a camera in the house doesn't feel comfortable, maybe you'd like to bring in help.

Bringing in Help

Ask, "Would you be okay with someone in the home to help out?" If having help is appealing, then you can work out the details and see if there's someone you both approve of. If the answer is yes, you want to determine what kind of person to find.

You can offer a health aide (watch out for the "I don't need a babysitter" comment). A companion to play cards or games, watch television, and go for walks. A personal assistant (look at me, I'm "fancy" now) can handle bookkeeping, errands, and tasks with/for your person. A chef, driver, or housekeeper makes life easier. A tech tutor or handyperson can provide a service and seem less like a babysitter. Hiring assistance in whatever form is about the same cost of hiring a health aide.

I met Dennis in my Home Health Aide course and discovered he had experience doing odd jobs for his last patient/client. Perfect. My mother had small projects she could create around the house, so we could leave Dennis painting and fixing things while Mom volunteered and shopped. I felt comfortable knowing that Dennis had CPR and first aid training. Dad liked that Dennis was a veteran (like Dad). Dennis would let me know if something went wrong and give me an idea of my dad's mental capacity after each visit. Dad didn't mind supervising the help and paying for a handyman to do my mother's projects. Dennis got paid for odd jobs for months, and we knew Dad had a certified home health aide on site.

Kitchen: If safety in the kitchen (leaving on the stove, cutting oneself on a knife, breaking glass jars, etc.) is on your mind, or you're afraid your loved one isn't eating, you could suggest that your loved one might benefit from a chef to cook meals. This keeps the kitchen safety from plaguing your dreams, and it sounds like you're offering a luxury benefit. You get someone checking in and talking with your loved one, thus providing socialization, resulting in healthier, fresher meals for your loved one that they'll eat.

Not interested in a chef but still need them not to cook? Offer to subscribe them to a meal delivery service. It can be supermarket delivery of premade meals or a chef-inspired delivery service with specific food goals and restrictions in mind.

Handyman: "Things around the house need to be repaired and kept up. What would you like fixed? I'll send someone in to take care of that."

Assistant: Can pay bills, handle household tasks, and run errands. My friend Rosemarie would visit her clients every two weeks or once a month to write their checks, calculate the balances, organize paperwork, track nonprofit donations, take them to the market, and order things on Amazon for her clients. She did their tech setup and called to resolve issues when there was a problem. Her clients sometimes didn't need that much done, but they loved the company and wanted Rosemarie to come anyway. Someone who can handle things for an aging person is less a guard dog and more a benefit.

Housekeeper: Comes like a hotel maid to clean the bathroom, bedroom, and kitchen until sparkling and no safety hazards are evident. This person can function in the background without bothering your loved one but also be a friend with whom to converse.

Companion: "(Fill in a name) needs company. Do you mind if I have someone stop by a few times a week to play cards and watch movies with you? They could also read a book to you."

LEAVING HOME

Before moving your loved one out of the home to a new community with care services, consider all available options. There are multiple ways to ensure your loved one is being watched over; and that someone is around to call you if there's a problem if you can't be on-site all the time.

A pro/con and expense comparisons will help make decision-making more practical. Some alternatives to moving out to offer your loved one:

- Become a roommate, perhaps in a friend's home, or invite a roommate into the existing home.
- Move from the current house to a smaller, easily manageable, safer apartment.
- Spend part of the year with one child and the other part with another until travel is untenable.
- Move closer to family.
- Travel full-time on a cruise ship.
- Move to a hotel.
- Move to a 55+community.
- Invite a college or nursing student to share the current house with your loved one.
- Invite a young person aging out of foster care to share the house.

The biggest lies aging people tell themselves are (a) I'll never need a nursing home and (b) When I get sick, I will live with/near my child. Technology and ease of travel have made it so that many family members live pretty far apart these days. Some cultures embrace caring for their aging relatives, sharing a home with them until the end. And sure, there are communities where multiple family members have homes near each other; that's when caregiving becomes accepted as a responsibility of the entire clan.

The idea of multiple generations sharing a home is not as common as it used to be. Individualism is more the norm. We all know it takes a village to raise a child, and I propose it takes a village to care for our aging and infirm. Support and community can make our so-called golden years a lot easier.

Making a big move means giving up the familiar and safe to head toward new and foreign. As we age, familiar equals good. Having to pack up your life, downsize, and go through all the memories and emotions attached to every individual thing is genuinely distressing to some and overwhelming to most. Resistance is the first line of defense.

Conversations around leaving home to move to independent or assisted living or investing in a continuing care community are never one-day discussions. It can take months or even years to find the right fit and for someone to agree to make this kind of move. Even moving to a 55+ community can bring on stress.

All the what-ifs come into play. What if the new place is uncomfortable? What if I don't know anyone or if I don't like anyone, or if no one likes me? What if I hate it there? Will anyone I know come to visit me?

Most people's instinct is, "I want to die at home. Leave me alone." Then, they defensively ask, "Why are you trying to take my home away from me?"

You become the enemy if you force someone to move before the decision is agreed upon. At some point, the physical condition of your loved one may influence a move. Deciding where to go before that happens is optimal, if not always possible.

If you're trying to move your parent(s), securing agreement among all the siblings is best before you talk with your parents. If one child wants the parents to stay in their own home and the other siblings want the parents to move, it becomes a tug of war: an us-against-them battle. "We all think this is best for you at this time" is a much better position to be in than one child wanting parents to move to her home, another wanting parents to move to a medically supported facility, and another wanting parents to stay put in his childhood home. It's confusing for your parents. It can be a who-do-you-love-most emotional battlefield where whichever idea your parent chooses is seen as a statement about favored child status.

Having a doctor, financial advisor, or elder law attorney be the "bad guy" can sometimes keep family harmony. Having a professional present the family with facts and opinions based on dealing with similar issues daily allows the family to point to professional advice as evidence for their concern.

Judy, my mother's ninety-year-old friend, was brought to a senior residence by her three sons to have lunch a few months after her husband, who used a wheelchair and had dementia, passed away. Judy tells the story that her boys said, "'This is where you live now. Here are the keys to your new apartment.' And they just left me there." Judy cautioned my mother when Mom shared my proposal for moving. I can pretty much guarantee that it wasn't like that, but that's how Judy is telling everyone her children treated her after the death of her husband. It would have been a different story recounted to my mother if Judy had agreed with her children about moving. (Judy ultimately met a lovely, handsome, and healthy man in her new community, got involved in a bunch of activities, became a volunteer, and settled in quite happily to her new life.)

The debate rages on whether waiting until the last moment or moving while you're still well and able is best. There are pros and cons for each. You'll potentially save money if you wait and stay home as long as possible. The environment is familiar and friendly. The routines are already set. You remain close to doctors, friends, service people, shops, etc. However, if you stay home, you could fall or get injured; perhaps no one will know. People have been lying on the floor for hours or even days with no one checking in.

We worried that if my father fell, the ceramic tile was so hard that (being on blood thinners) he could wind up bleeding to death if his head hit the tile or he might fracture a hip. One day, he slid off the chair on his terrace and couldn't stand up again; he forgot how. He sat on the floor for over an hour until my mother came home and found him out there.

The physical environment at home may be unsafe: Climbing over a bathtub to get into a shower, outdated and possibly dangerous appliances, and roofs/doors/windows needing repair, are all things to explore. Consider the what-if scenarios and home safety factors during a storm or emergency needing backup power. Think about when things are not perfectly ideal.

When two people are together, moving as a couple is much easier than waiting for one to pass and then moving a newly single person into strange surroundings. After losing a spouse, compounding the stress by having to pack up a home, going through the move with boxes to unpack and setting up everything in a different environment, trying to make new friends when desolate over a recent loss, eating foods prepared in an unfamiliar manner, and generally being surrounded by everything alien is a quick ride down a spiral staircase headed straight to Dangerland.

I made a significant case to my parents: "What happens to Mom if Dad passes first? Mom will be left on her own with no one to take care of or talk to. She will be lonely and depressed, and I fear she will be miserable." Dad did not want that. Even though Dad loved his view and liked to be alone in the apartment while Mom ran around town, he knew Mom was a social person with a need for contact and new people to talk to all the time. He was primarily antisocial, preferring his own company since he had started losing his hearing. Mom was driving him up the wall, being at home all day, and picking on him because she had no distractions.

Physically, Mom needed daily exercise classes. The challenge proffered was a new residence with everything social and healthy for her and a water view for him. Dad responded, "It's not going to be easy to convince me, but if you find a place you think I can tolerate for your mother, I will agree to look." He gave me a list of standards, confident that I wouldn't be able to find what he wanted.

Oh boy—when I found everything he asked for, he admitted that it was pretty spectacular and that if he was going to move, I had found the right place. Of course, there were some runner-up facilities, where he said he would throw up every time he walked in the door if I made him move there. Similar to searching for a spouse/partner… you have to experience a few losers until you find the perfect match.

This was a big surprise to Dad that he found a place he liked. They moved. And later, when he was occasionally depressed about not being in his familiar home, he said, "I'm not mad at you. I know I made this decision for your mother's happiness. I will make it work for your mother." FYI: My mother was *so* happy there that she said if Dad wanted to move out, she wasn't going anywhere!

When Dad passed away four years into living there, the community went out of its way to be gracious to my mother. Mom had people constantly coming to her to offer condolences, inviting her to activities, and dining with her. She thanks my siblings and me frequently for foreseeing that this would be the best thing for her.

When someone needs more care, you'll want to look at independent living, assisted living, memory care, or skilled nursing, depending on the wellness of the individual(s) moving. Wherever you pick, ensure that someone can stay in the same place when their physical or cognitive wellness becomes more challenged.

When you are have multiple rationales why someone needs to move, maybe don't share everything at once, but over time, drop hints.

I've offered some conversation starter points for you to consider but you will find additional points that are relevant to your specific situation, I am sure. Don't wait until a decision is no longer an option because a move is required for the person's safety.

Physical

- ❖ "You can't walk that well anymore. What if you fall? Will someone be around to lift you if you're here at home alone? Wouldn't it be nice to be in a place where everyone is trained to help; where doctors, nurses, and physical therapists are around to help you and answer your questions?"

- ❖ "There's a pull cord in this new apartment that can bring you emergency help if you need it."
- ❖ "Everything in the new apartment is set up to prevent falls and tripping so you can remain independent. It's built to accommodate a wheelchair or walker if needed. There are grab bars, unique easy-to-turn handles, protection for the temperature of the water, no-slip floors, cushioned flooring in case you do fall, raised cabinets with doors that can easily be removed, shower seating, etc. We all will feel much calmer knowing you are in a safer residence."
- ❖ "If you want to stay in your home, we must make some extensive safety renovations. That could get costly and inconvenient for you with construction dust, drilling, hammering, and jackhammering, which could last for a few weeks, a month, a few months, etc., and I/we think you'll be miserable going through that alone." (You might accompany this with a list of the repairs/updates that would be needed, how much they might cost, and how long it will take to do each one.)

Security

- ❖ "If you don't come down to eat, someone will come looking for you in a community instead of you being on your own. Don't you want to know that someone is watching out for you? Someone cares? I want to know I can call and send someone to find you if I can't reach you."
- ❖ "I/we don't like you driving around all the time. What if you get lost or have something happen to you? Isn't it easier to have someone drive you? At this new place, they have a driver on call to take you places, and they have bus trips to shop and go for entertainment so you can go with a group of people and maybe make some new friends!"
- ❖ "We get nervous when you're out or home on your own. What if you get attacked? Who will watch over you while we are out of town or busy with work? If you don't want to move out, we should put in a security camera. One on the outside and one inside the house. We want to know you're safe."
- ❖ "If you have a reaction to your medicine, your blood sugar gets too low, or you feel faint, I feel better knowing someone can assist you."

Financial

- ❖ "Owning your own home is expensive. Things break down. You won't have to worry about that anymore. You pay all these different monthly expenses and will need (new appliances, water heater fixed, AC replaced, dying tree removed, etc.), which will cost big bucks. Wouldn't you rather use your money for things you enjoy?"
- ❖ "You'll have an in-house handyman for anything that goes wrong."
- ❖ "Your memory isn't what it used to be, and I can see it's getting more difficult for you to manage all your bills. Wouldn't it be nice to know you have one bill to pay each month and everything is included?
- ❖ "I understand you would rather be in your home with a part-time aide. You don't need a full-time aide right now, but you might someday. A full-time aide costs $25 an hour, about $80,000 a year. A live-in aide will cost $40,000 to $80,000 a year, and you must find a substitute if they get sick, need a vacation, have a family crisis, and need to leave. Plus, you still need to pay the ongoing household expenses. That can be very stressful for you (me) to manage."

Emotional/Spiritual

- "I know your friends are passing away or moving. It's hard to deal with that alone. We'd like for you to be somewhere that has activities and new people for you to meet. You haven't made any new friends in a while here at home. Aren't you feeling lonely?"
- "If you moved in with us (the response they offer as to why they won't be lonely) (a) we're at work/school and out all the time. (b) You'll be bored and have no one to talk to. (c) Our home has too many steps/levels/animals running around that could make getting around more difficult."
- "The place we are recommending for you believes in supporting people's spiritual lives. You would make friends who also want spiritual observance. They offer (a) Religious services on-site. You can go every day/week if you like. (b) The driver/van will take you to services where you like to go."
- "You must be getting bored doing the same thing all the time. Wouldn't having someone else plan exciting activities and trips for you be nice? You will get to do all these cool things someone else plans, and they handle all the details!" Alternatively (if your loved one is an organizer), "Think of all the great activities you can plan for all your new friends and neighbors!" or "Imagine how your new neighbors and friends would love learning all about (insert favorite activity or skill)."
- "You can share your talent for (fill in) with the other residents at the new place. They would be so happy to have someone with your skill/talent."
- "You've always wanted a (pool, walking trail, movie theater, massage therapist) and the place we'd like to show you has that plus (theater trips, casino buses, cooking classes, gardening program, etc.)."
- "While you're fully able to, wouldn't you like to get to know the staff and the benefits of your new home? Do you want to wake up one day in a strange place when you're sick and not know anyone, not knowing how to get around, not knowing the schedule? I think it would be best if you weren't a nervous wreck in addition to being overwhelmed!"

NOTES:

(a) An investment in a continuing care community (CCC) guarantees that residential and medical needs will all be taken care of for life at a low monthly rent from the day you move in.

(b) Long-Term Care Insurance will cover you at home for medical expenses but not household expenses, and there are often limits to how much they'll cover—based on the policy purchased.

Guilt (It's not like your loved one/parents never pulled the guilt card on you!)

- "I am so worried about you and your safety that it impacts my life."
- "My relationship with (my spouse, partner, ability to date) is challenging because I spend all my spare energy and time checking in on you. Do you want me to be alone?"
- "I can't take a vacation because I always use my time off to be with you."
- "My job is being affected. I can't travel… (missing meetings, can't put in the hours I need, too distracted to get work done correctly, etc.)"
- "The stress of worrying about your health and safety is causing me to have health problems. Now I worry that if I get sick, who will be here to help look after you?"
- "It would be easier for me to just come visit you and enjoy time together instead of me trying to manage your home and health in every conversation."
- "I've gone through my life savings over this last (insert how much time), and I can't afford to continue caring for you full-time. I need to go back to work and replenish my finances."

Once they are open to exploring, ask what they want in a new space. What does it have to have to make them happy? Ask about lifestyle, physical layout, amenities, activities, other residents, animals, décor style, etc. Making a list of the "perfect" place could get someone excited the way making a list of how you'd spend your lottery winnings brings cheer to your soul.

- "I/we want *you* to choose where you'd like to be. You should never feel that I/we are pushing you into a place you don't like because of your current and future health."
- "While you can still decide, why don't I take you to a few places I've already screened that meet your criteria, and you can choose the one you like? We can discuss when would be best to move in after you make your selection. Maybe it will be soon, or maybe it will be when we reach certain milestones that we can set together regarding your health/finances, etc."

Once the idea of moving is starting to pique an interest, it's your job to do research on your own or call a relocation person, senior placement person, or online service to narrow the choices and come up with a list of places to visit.

Part 2

CONVERSATION TIPS FOR COMMUNICATING WITH AGING ADULTS

General Aging
Cognitively Challenged/Dementia
Navigating Public Outings
Relationship Building with Doctors

COMMUNICATING WITH AGING LOVED ONES

For years my mother had a habit of talking to my father as she walked from room to room. She would start asking a question as she approached him and finish it with her head in the refrigerator or sitting on the toilet in the bathroom. (TMI?) My father heard, "Honey, would you like mmghphon?" and he would get agitated. She may have been asking if he wanted his favorite shrimp cocktail appetizer or if he wanted a prostate exam—my dad didn't know. So, he got angry. Mom complained that Dad never answered her questions and would stop talking to her or stomp off somewhere. Quality communication is simply making a connection that can be heard and understood.

More complicated communication comes when you want your loved one to do something they stubbornly do not want to do, like showering. Rosemarie learned that if she phrased her request to her mother as "You said you wanted to take a shower. Do you want to do that now or after lunch?" instead of, "Mom, you need to take a shower." The decision-making has changed, and the behavior is no longer if but when, which makes a big difference in caregiving. In sales, they call that an assumptive close.

The Louis and Anne Green Memory & Wellness Center in Boca Raton, Florida, recommends the following for clear communication:

- Do not talk until you are face-to-face.
- Speak clearly and in concise, simple, short sentences.
- Allow your loved one time to respond, as it may take them longer to process information.
- Use gestures when appropriate.
- Give your loved one every opportunity to express themselves.
- Be a creative listener; listen to the meaning behind words.
- Do not argue over the correct answer.
- Use "I" statements instead of "you" when/if you become angry.
- Continue talking about things that are important to your loved one.
- Monitor and modify your tone of voice, body language, and other communication methods.

If you've made an effort to be present and speak clearly and still have trouble getting your point across or get an angry response, remind yourself that often, a person's confusion has to do with their disease/symptoms (hard of hearing, blurred vision, confusion, foggy brain, etc.) and not their feelings about you. Be patient.

Reading Behaviors as Clues for Information[1]

As loved ones age, you might see behaviors that seem different than their norm. Try looking at all behaviors as a form of communication. Understand that acting out may not be personally directed at you but might be a call for attention about something your loved one is trying to tell you.

Out-of-the-norm behavior means you need to investigate. Like a baby crying or a dog barking, new behaviors may indicate that your loved one is trying to tell you something but can't find the words. Perhaps he has to go to the bathroom, has a tummy ache, or is hungry. She is tired and wants to go to bed, wants something to drink, has an itch, or needs a hug. Take a moment to note when the behaviors appear and ask questions to identify the cause.

New behaviors you might see your loved one exhibit as they age or become cognitively or physically challenged include giddiness, aggression, withdrawal, anxiety, agitation, confusion, paranoia, repetition, trouble with sleep or wanting to sleep all the time, wandering off, forgetfulness, depression, inappropriate sexual advances, hallucinating, hiding things, and so on.

Causes and Response

If a behavior change occurs suddenly, consider getting your loved one a test for a urinary tract infection. A UTI is a common cause of agitated behavior, sudden fatigue, increased confusion, and more. Left untreated, a UTI can lead to other health and behavioral issues. A quick urine analysis will tell you if a simple dose of antibiotics will eliminate the problem.

If not a UTI, keep looking for physical causes if the behavior is out of character. You know your loved one best, so don't give up if you see something you know to be unusual.

Jorrie's father suddenly began cursing at her, telling her she was a horrible daughter, pointing out every flaw, insisting on attention and immediate gratification in the form of food and snacks. Requests, demands, and commands were shouted from in front of the TV in another room. This was unlike his usual grateful, amiable self. Jorrie took her dad to the doctor, and many tests later discovered that her father had a brain tumor.

At a doctor's office one day, in the waiting room, Maddie's mother reached out and banged the side of her hand against Maddie's arm—chop, chop, chop—repeatedly, violently, causing pain. Maddie couldn't get her mother to stop hitting her. Maddie gave one chop back on her mother's arm, the same strength her mother was using, and her mother retreated and yelped, "Ouch!"

Maddie said, "That's what you're doing to me! Stop it. It hurts."

Her mother looked at her sadly, with the eyes of an innocent child, and said, "I was just playing. I'm sorry."

Maddie feels tremendous guilt and shame over her reaction, perhaps the same way a parent feels about giving a child a smack on the bottom or when we tap the nose of a dog that is putting his face into the trash. It is not something any of us ever want to deal with. We are human, and we react instantly. Knowing that

---

[1] Alzheimer's Association free brochure called "Behaviors"

hitting is an indication of something else might have made Maddie react differently. Perhaps Maddie wasn't paying enough attention to her mother while they were in a place her mother found scary or confusing (the doctor's office).

Negative behaviors may be related to:

- ❖ Physical pain
- ❖ Temperature discomfort
- ❖ Overstimulation
- ❖ Unfamiliar surroundings
- ❖ Complicated tasks
- ❖ Frustrating interactions because of the inability to communicate
- ❖ Urinary Tract Infection or other health issue

To Change the Behavior

Step I: Examine the behavior.

Once you rule out pain (constipation, gas, an infection, an injury), a UTI, or a medication reaction as the cause of new or harmful behavior, first, try not to take the behaviors personally and then look for solutions.

However, if the new behavior turns to striking or biting or leads to self-harming activities, call the doctor immediately for help unveiling the cause. Focus on keeping your loved one and yourself safe.

Step II: Explore potential solutions.

Work on calmly distracting or diverting your loved one from the situation that triggered the behavior. Speak slowly, make eye contact, use a gentle touch to connect (but don't startle by coming from the sides or behind), provide reassurance, and focus on something new.

Try inviting your loved one to help you with something they are physically able to do without difficulty (folding laundry, setting the table, drying dishes), something uncomplicated and familiar will usually work. Begin a song or dance. Start playing a game, pull out a jigsaw puzzle, or read a soothing and uncomplicated book aloud. Do something creative like painting or flower arranging. Start sketching or coloring. Visit the garden. Bring in an animal (live or robot[2]) to embrace and talk to.

Ask your loved one a question about something from the past to prompt a story: Ask Dad, "Where did you meet Mom?" Ask your spouse, "Who was your best friend when you were little?" Ask your friend, "What was your favorite childhood game?" Whatever catches your loved one's interest and attention.

An example: A common frustration is when you have a doctor's appointment and your loved one stubbornly refuses to get dressed. Instead of fighting to get your loved one to put on clothing, try to divert your

---

[2] JoyforAll.com robot pets

loved one to another activity (like eating or packing a purse or activity bag) and then come back to getting dressed when things calm down.

> Note: Scheduling enough extra time for potential drama and challenges will help keep you calmer and less frustrated.

Step III: Try various responses.

Use the KISS method. The US Navy created this acronym for "Keep it simple, stupid." The idea is that things often work best if they are kept simple rather than made complicated.

Offer only one alternative. When preparing a meal, instead of asking, "What would you like for dinner?" make it simple by asking, "Would you like a hamburger or baked chicken?"

Break tasks into smaller steps. Just supply instructions one (maximum two) step at a time. For getting dressed, you might say, "Here are your socks. Can you put them on, please?" and wait until the socks are on before handing them a T-shirt. When that's on, give them the slacks/shorts/skirt. And so on. Laying everything out on the bed and expecting someone to understand what order and how to put it all on can be overwhelming and could result in arms crossed and refusal to move.

Speak face-to-face. Conversations from the side or behind someone can be confusing and frightening (especially if there are vision or hearing losses). Accents and mumbling add to the confusion, so speak slowly where lips can be read. Allow your intention to be interpreted from your facial expression by speaking at eye level, face-to-face.

Sometimes, it's not the words but the face and tone that make a difference. You can say the most inconsequential thing, but if you do it in a singsong talking-to-a-child voice, your loved one might take it as insulting their intelligence. If you smile while saying something difficult, the listener's mood might be better than if the same thing is said with gloom, or wincing, or so hurriedly the person can't hear it.

Use short sentences with simple words that get straight to the point, but don't talk down to an aging parent or spouse as if to a child. Avoid baby talk or letting resentment and annoyance show.

Try the simple "Let's go to the store" instead of an overwhelming list of things you need to get that day. Don't run through the menu for the week or what you're eating on which night. "Tonight, I thought I'd prepare your favorite: spaghetti." As your loved one's ability to focus begins to waiver, continue to simplify your language.

TEN COMMUNICATION ABSOLUTES

Unless we are doctors, therapists, or experienced professional caregivers, we should admit we don't always know what we're dealing with. However, unlike professionals, you know if your parent or loved one's behaviors are out of the norm. As stated in the last section, if behavior changes occur suddenly, first see if there's a medical or mental health issue. If all comes out clear, examine the behavior and try various responses.

This great placard is a tool that summarizes Jo Huey's 10 Absolutes to copy into your smartphone notes section or computer to remind you of more positive ways to interact with those you care about or customers/clients with oncoming cognitive issues. This was written for Alzheimer's patients, but I think it's practical for anyone from small children up through people at the later stages of life.

> Note: As you read through this practical advice, consider how it might improve any partnership or marriage situation, too.

Alzheimer's Communication

1. Never **Argue**. Instead **Agree**.

2. Never **Reason**. Instead **Divert**.

3. Never **Shame**. Instead **Distract**.

4. Never **Lecture**. Instead **Reassure**.

5. Never say "**Remember**." Instead **Reminisce**.

6. Never say "**I Told You**." Instead **Repeat**.

7. Never say "**You Can't**." Instead say what they **Can Do**.

8. Never **Demand**. Instead **Ask**.

9. Never **Condescend**. Instead **Encourage**.

10. Never **Force**. Instead **Reinforce**.

COMMUNICATION WITH THE GENERAL PUBLIC

About Your Loved One's Challenges

For me, the most challenging time of this dementia journey was when my dad was kind of with- it most of the time, when he was aware of what people saw and thought on some core level. My instinct was always to protect him, to honor the person he had always been.

For others, there are physical behaviors that may be attention-drawing. There are moments when you're out in public ordering at the deli counter, sitting at a restaurant table, or waiting for public transport, and you observe people staring. Maybe your dad starts shaking uncontrollably, but if you shout, "Hey, my dad has Parkinson's! He's not drunk! Give us a break!" you'll risk embarrassing him more, right? Or your aunt tries to hug someone in the aisle at Target because she's feeling happy: "No, Aunt Carol is not coming on to you; she's got Alzheimer's."

Your loved one is likely to have a meltdown listening to you trying to explain them to a stranger. You're embarrassed. They're embarrassed. And the public doesn't know what to do with this information.

Julie's mother stood in an Italian restaurant, turned to the other diners, and began singing an Italian aria from a favorite opera. She then thanked her fans for coming to see her! Julie's mom had been a professional opera singer in her younger years, and her voice was still remarkable, so at least there was that. And it *was* an Italian restaurant. Julie hurried her mother out of the restaurant as her mother continued to wave like Miss America on a parade float. You never know what will happen sometimes!

A simple, inexpensive tip to help in these situations is to carry around a business card that says something to the effect of ", *My mother/father/husband/friend has Alzheimer's/ Dementia/ Parkinson's. Please be patient.* You can do this for symptoms, too. *Hearing Loss: Please speak slowly, face-to-face, and at a higher volume. Vision Loss: Please don't make quick moves or try to touch my mother/father/spouse.*

The Alzheimer's Association has cards that say: *My companion has Alzheimer's disease. This is a brain disorder that makes communication difficult. Your patience and understanding are greatly appreciated. Thank you.*

You can add information about your loved one and whatever behaviors someone might see that could startle or scare a stranger:

- ❖ Sometimes, she answers slowly.
- ❖ My companion may appear confused.
- ❖ My companion gets easily upset.
- ❖ My companion may shake uncontrollably.
- ❖ My companion can get overly affectionate.

Customize your message. Keep it short and to the point.

You can purchase cards from others who have done this on various websites. If you want to customize your own card, you can go to your local print shop or online printers to get cards printed in bulk.

Only need a few? You can buy blank business cards to run through your home printer. You can purchase packages of blank business or postcards from any office supply store or big box store with a business department, usually sold near the printers. These cards come with instructions and guide sheets to walk you through how to set this up on your computer and print them as needed. Homemade cards are easier to update as things change.

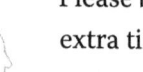

I'm with someone with Alzheimer's.
Please be patient, as he needs
extra time to make decisions.

COMMUNICATING WITH DOCTORS/CLINICIANS

Tamara (a former New Yorker whose mother and father lived in Florida) and I were commiserating about our experiences with doctors and how they react to our parents. We've both experienced the condescending doctor who talks as if the aging patient is a child; the officious doctor who does not take a moment to talk but instead conducts the exam at lightning speed, perhaps to be able to bill as many visits as possible or doesn't apologize for being late or making people wait; the doctor who sees the patient is having trouble understanding and turns away and starts to talk to you as though the patient isn't in the room at all. And then there's the kind of doctor who asks questions, talks to the patient, explains things in easy-to-understand language, and provides written follow-up instructions. Don't lose professionals in this latter group. I have been blessed to include many of them on my parents' care team.

Since Tamara had just moved her parents closer to her in Georgia and was now becoming a more active advocate and caregiver for them, she asked me, "What if you have a parent who doesn't truly comprehend what is going on but believes they do? You don't want to embarrass your parent by taking over the physician visit, but you know that the doctor needs to have certain information, and you have questions that need to be answered. How do you manage this situation?"

My friend Barb in Connecticut asked a similar question. Her parents live in Louisiana, and she wanted to know how she could do follow-up for her parents if the doctors would not provide accurate, current information to her, and yet her parents didn't feel that they needed any help so they wouldn't share either.

My process applies even if your spouse or loved one doesn't recognize their limitations.

I spoke with my parents before we went to see doctors and before health issues started worsening to let them know that I wanted to be sure they get the best care and that as long as I know what's going on and the doctors share with me too, I can be there for them (my parents). They can relax knowing they can always ask me if they forget something or have more questions.

I told Tamara my parents know they are forgetting, so this makes them feel better without embarrassing them. I'm functioning like a human backup memory drive, if you will. And because I shared my intention to be a helper and not to become my parents' "boss," they were most happy to have me there. My parents often turned to me to ask, "What did I tell you was wrong the other day? I can't remember."

I then shared with Tamara the conversation starter I use with the doctors. In front of my parents, I tell the doctors that I am there as my parents' helper and advocate and that my parents are afraid that they might forget something. "If my parents have a question later," I tell the doctors, "As long as I understand everything as we're going through the visit, then I can (a) help ensure they follow through where they are supposed to and (b) answer my parents' questions when they don't remember or understand, instead of my parents calling your office again." The doctors love this. I sit, take notes, and sometimes ask clarifying questions while the doctors talk to my parents.

If you don't live near your loved one, you can ask to be on speakerphone during the doctor's visit. COVID-19 taught us how to participate in visits remotely. My sister or brother in New York could be there for Mom or Dad at the doctor's office in Florida if I had a conflicting appointment or deadline. I can now be on the phone when my sister is at the doctor's in New York with my mother.

If you are there, paying attention, when a parent provides wrong information or forgets to tell something to the doctor, you can speak up and share, "Mom, didn't you say that you felt a little dizzy a few days ago and that you wanted to tell the doctor?" And then Mom can take over and tell the story.

"Dad, you said you are depressed about your situation these days. Do you want to tell the doctor what that feels like to you so maybe she can help?" Dad can decide if he wants to share, but at least the doctor has heard that there may be an issue and can ask guiding questions during the rest of the exam.

Write down everything the doctor says. After the visit, you can review it slowly with your loved one and put the follow-up appointments and medication times on your loved one's calendar and to-do list.

My parents felt relief that they didn't have to remember and understand everything. They had me as their backup, their safety net. I logged all their appointments into a shared calendar on our iPhones and set the reminder function so my parents and I would know when they had something coming up. Doing this also gave me historical visit information in case the medical staff or doctor needed to know.

Communicating pain to family, doctors, or clinicians

If your loved one is acting out and might be in pain, using a pain scale may give them a way to tell you how they're feeling and indicate to a doctor just how bad the pain is. Pointing to what hurts on the body or in a photo of a body form also helps.

This Wong-Baker FACES® Pain Rating Scale is used worldwide to help people communicate pain levels. Show your loved one the faces and have them pick the one that matches how they feel. (Go to http://wong-bakerfaces.org for more information about the pain scale and incredible organization.)

Wong-Baker FACES® Pain Rating Scale

0	2	4	6	8	10
No Pain	A Little Pain	A Little More Pain	Even More Pain	A Whole Lot Of Pain	Worst Pain

©1983 Wong-Baker FACES Foundation. www.WongBakerFACES.org
Used with permission.

Tracking Pain

From the Wong-Baker Organization, Connie Baker suggested that caregivers might find a **Pain Relief Log** useful for tracking information to share at doctor visits. "It is a way of keeping a record of vital information like pain meds, pain assessment, and anything else they want to track. Great for continuity of care." Connie offers a Pain Relief Log document for free by entering your contact information here: https://wongbaker-faces.org/wong-baker-faces-pain-relief-log.

When someone is cognitively challenged or has some issue that makes speaking a challenge, try communicating by using a card system, such as Caregiver Cards—Picture-Based Communication Cue Cards for Adults with Memory, Speech, and Cognitive Challenges. Created by Caregiver Cards, this is a series of player cards in a deck that allows someone who finds speaking a challenge to pick out what is troubling them. By holding up the card or pointing at it, they can let someone know where they might be having an issue.

These cards cover physical as well as emotional issues. Knowing someone feels depressed, anxious, or in pain can help you find a resolution instead of just seeing someone miserable and not knowing what is causing the unease. Bringing these cards to the doctor can help, but it's probably better to go through them before you get to the doctor so you can relay the findings.

GO BAG AND TOOL KITS FOR A LESS STRESSED HOSPITAL STAY

When a woman is pregnant, it is expected that as she approaches her due date, she has a packed bag that can be grabbed when she enters labor and heads out for the birthing space or hospital. Since it's more likely than not that an aging person will need a hospital stay at some point, you can be prepared in advance by having everything that will be needed packed and ready to go. This pre-packed bag will make your life less stressful and significantly increase the hospital staff's ability to provide care in the most beneficial and comforting way possible. Should you need to "pick up a few things at the house for me" when someone enters rehab for example, having this bag packed eliminates the need for you to root around in people's private things, as it also reduces the fear that you forgot something important.

In addition to all the medical information your doctor would have—and that you should have with you anyway—here are some suggestions for extra things you might want packed for a hospital stay:

Emergency Information – Things you might need with you: health information, medical contacts, insurance documents, legal ID, legal forms, DNR/DNI notarized form, citizen documents, and organ donation card.

Tool Kit – A bag filled with items to keep you or the patient comfortable and calm while waiting for visits, doctors, examinations, and tests.

Some items I include: a shawl, blanket, sweater, socks, comfortable shoes/slippers, music, headset, writing paper and pens, coloring books and markers/pencils, deck of cards, compliant healthy snacks, refillable spill-proof water bottle, tea bags or tea/fruit diffuser bottle, refillable mug with cap, and a few dollars of change or prepaid debit card for vending machines.

Personal Information Sheet – Type a Personal Information Sheet before your visit and ask the medical staff to keep it with your loved one's chart. Use bullet points with short, bold headings. You might include your loved one's routine (wake/sleep times, breakfast habits, coffee/tea preferences, etc.), how to address the patient (formal or informal), personal habits, likes and dislikes, any trigger behaviors that might cause a reaction and the best way to respond. Include any nonverbal signs the patient is prone to exhibit in pain or discomfort, likely reactions to touch, and what tickles. If your loved one has hearing aids or needs glasses or any other assistance, that should be included.

Let the team know your parents' level of dementia (if any) so the nurses can tell the difference between hospital delirium[3] and dementia.

---

[3] Mayo Clinic has information to define delirium vs. dementia: http://www.mayoclinic.org/diseases-conditions/delirium/symptoms-causes/syc-20371386

When Can We Talk?

Sample

Personal Information Sheet For _____

My Normal Routine/Personal Habits:

_____
_____
_____
_____
_____
_____

I prefer to be addressed:

☐ Formally ☐ Mr. ☐ Ms. ☐ Mrs. _____

☐ Informally Nickname: _____ First name: _____

Things I like: _____
Things I dislike: _____
Ticklish spots: _____

Notes: ☐ I have hearing aids ☐ I wear glasses ☐ I have contact lenses

Other assistance I may need:

_____
_____
_____
_____
_____

Part 3

YOUR SUPPORT/ CARE TEAM

Siblings
Experts/Professionals
Support Group
Neighbors and Friends

CREATING A CARE TEAM

We only have twenty-four hours in any day. There are only so many days in a week, month, and year. The number of tasks and responsibilities for caregivers is so extensive that it feels like there's never enough time to collect yourself. You can get overwhelmed (been there, done that), or you can get smart about it and attack this like any other job with resources you can activate to get the job done more efficiently, with better outcomes. That's where I am now. That doesn't mean I don't collapse and cry and whine to anyone who will listen sometimes, but for the most part, I'm keeping it together and getting better and better at finding time for myself within the scope of work that needs to be done.

What I've come to realize is that I am not a superhero. This may surprise some who know me because people think I have it all together. Ha! That's what I want them to think. But I know that I can't do this all alone. I suspect you know this, too. Nor do we want to, right?

The longer I'm caregiving, the more I am convinced that trying to be a superhero is detrimental to your well-being. We need supporters who can either help take tasks off our plate, provide respite time for us to recover, or handle errands so we can take time for personal care. We don't want to feel isolated and lonely when we're giving our all to caregiving.

Your support team could comprise professionals with expertise for which you pay. It could be in support groups where people share and allow you to unburden but also where you will find answers and advice from others facing similar challenges. It might be neighbors or friends who don't mind adding a few things to their shopping list or making a stop or two for you when doing errands. Or it may be your family, your siblings, for example, who pull together to share a caregiving burden.

This section includes advice on setting up a network, creating your support team, and activating your team to get some needed respite and reduce your burden. With this in hand, let go of any guilt you might harbor for needing help. Asking for help is wise and will mean that you can be selfless and continue caregiving with more energy for as long as needed.

Getting Started

Before you can pull together a team, knowing what you will ask for is helpful. Grab a piece of paper or create a spreadsheet to start a chart on your computer. This can be as simple as folding a letter-size paper into four. Create headings at the top of the columns for How often/Task/How long it takes/Who can help.

Then, list everything you need to do daily, weekly, and monthly for yourself and your loved one for whom you are providing care. Begin when you wake up and finish when you go to sleep. Itemize *everything*! Once you have the list of all you do, then break it down. What goes into getting all those things done each day for yourself and the person you are providing care for?

If you start with something as simple as brushing teeth, that involves having toothpaste and a toothbrush in the bathroom, a clean towel, a cup for water, etc. The steps for this will create a task list that would include keeping toothpaste in the house, doing laundry for towels, and cleaning and rinsing cups regularly.

Eating food breaks down to making meals, so you need to buy groceries, then cook, prepare, or order food from somewhere.

Getting dressed involves having clothing suitable for the climate, which means buying clothing and accessories, keeping clothing clean and mended, putting clothing in the closet, dresser, or armoire, selecting what to wear, and getting dressed. To keep clothing clean, you must buy laundry detergent and do the wash, dry, and fold routine.

Once you complete this chart/list, you can start to figure out who you can ask to help transfer some of those things off your plate to theirs. Assigning someone a single task or request is far more likely to get cooperation than the generic "I could use some help." Those words are scary. *How long will they need me? How much will it cost? What if I don't know how to do what they ask?*

A request to pick up laundry detergent and socks at the market is much more specific than "Can you help me this morning?"

Asking someone to prepare three meals for lunch and drop them off in microwavable containers is more manageable than saying something more general like, "I need help with meals."

Asking someone if they can do a few loads of laundry is specific. Asking someone to "Help around the house" is indeterminate.

And when someone offers three hours of free time, what can they do to help? You will have a list of everything you need done. They can choose the things they are most comfortable completing, and you can check those off your list for the day/week/month.

Sample Chart

HOW OFTEN	TASK	HOW LONG IT TAKES	WHO CAN HELP
Weekly	Buy Groceries	1 hour	Neighbor (Sue)
Monthly	Pick up Prescriptions	½ hour	Work friend (Bob – lives near the pharmacy)
3 x Week	Laundry	1 hour per load	Daughter
Daily	Giving Bath/Shower	1 hour	Hired Aide
Daily	Getting Mom Dressed	½ hour	Hired Aide
Daily	Reading Mom the Newspaper	45 minutes	Book club friends rotating: M, T, W, Th, F

HOW OFTEN	TASK	HOW LONG IT TAKES	WHO CAN HELP
Daily	Going for a walk with Mom in wheelchair	45 minutes	Hired Aide or Granddaughter
Daily	Prepare Breakfast	15 minutes	Me
Daily	Serve Breakfast	30 minutes	Hired Aide
Daily	Prepare Lunch	15 minutes	Pre-packed by church ladies for the week
Daily	Serve Lunch	30 minutes	Hired Aide
Weekly	Pay Bills	20 minutes	Brother

Once you have the list, you can itemize the things that can be done by businesses you pay, what can be done by people you hire, and what can be completed with the help of generous volunteers and assigned to family members.

Naturally, when funds are limited, the volunteers and family become most critical. And when funds are limited, more efficient use of time becomes critical. If you can make all the lunches on Sunday, you save that prep time for the rest of the week. If you collect all the bills into one envelope and pay them at night, once a week, while watching television, you can free up time during the day to do things with your loved one.

Getting into routines and habits will also reduce the sense of being overwhelmed because you know it doesn't have to get done right now because it's on the schedule to get done at the end of the week at X time.

Getting organized and planning leaves room for the unexpected that invariably arrives. You avoid feeling crushed by piled-on responsibilities if everything is delegated to a time, resource, and budget.

CO-CAREGIVING – EMPOWERING OTHERS TO ASSIST

When I began my parental caregiving journey, it was my choice to relocate to Florida to be near my parents. I never anticipated all the levels of care that would be needed. I needed help. I turned to my siblings.

This concept of creating a Care Team is not just for siblings, though I write about that a lot here. Any collective of people interested in caring for someone can be part of a Care Team, so keep that in mind.

When I arrived in the summer of 2016, I immediately focused on logistics and the what-if stuff and began assessing everything. How was my parents' health? Their finances and taxes? Their paperwork needed to be converted from New York to Florida law. The condo was okay for the short term but wouldn't work if mobility became an issue. I recognized driving was an issue after a few shopping trips in the car with Mom.

The basics of elder care legal documentation and financial security were handled almost immediately because I could hire experts. I couldn't rely on truth in advertising, so I did some outreach, attended conferences and daylong events, watched webinars and lectures, and read reviews to find recommendations and advice when interviewing prospective estate and elder care lawyers and financial advisors. What questions should I ask? What should I look for? What do I need to do immediately, and what might I do some day in the future? How much was this going to cost? What were the laws around all this paperwork?

Then came the myriad of things that I never anticipated. There were so many tiny things that my siblings, still in New York, could not help with. I couldn't just turn to my sister and ask her to take Mom to the doctor so I could take Dad to the bank. I couldn't ask my brother to handle the contractor adding bathroom grab bars. My siblings, fortunately for me, wanted to be involved. "What can we do from here?" they asked at every call. So how do you gain that kind of cooperation and support from your siblings or other friends/family who could help? And how do you devise a delegation plan so everyone can be part of the team and feel like they're contributing? I joined a support group to find answers.

In my caregiver support group, I met people who were the primary caregivers (like me) and some who were long-distance caregivers. The long-distance caregivers had a different level of stress. More from not knowing what was going on. Feelings of guilt that they weren't close enough to help or that the burden was all on one person when they wished they could lighten that load. They often couldn't participate in every decision and action because they wouldn't know about it until after the moment passed. I honor that commitment and the love I knew they felt. There are challenges in both primary and secondary caregiving.

Some caregivers also have restricted emotional capacity, limited time or resources, and could only help indirectly and be backup support if/when needed. I feel that whatever someone can contribute should be welcomed. Caregiving can easily be a lonely road, and shutting people out only worsens the emotional stress.

One of us is always the primary caregiver. Whether local or not, the primary handles the thousands of little things. Often, one person is "good at the money stuff" and takes on that responsibility. Someone else might be in the health, finance, or legal fields and can take on that. But what can the printer, schoolteacher, restaurant owner, secretary, bartender, executive, or taxi driver do when they're not local? Turns out a lot. The key is that everyone can be part of the **Care Team** if a communication plan is implemented.

Creating a Caregiving Communication Plan

As in all matters between two or more people in any situation, the more you focus on clarity, the better the feelings of satisfaction and increased connectedness between all parties. To create a caregiving care team, you must answer the following questions first. After the list, read on for explanations for each question.

Questions to ask:

1) Who needs to be included in the communications?
2) How often does information need to be shared?
3) What kind of communication is preferred?
4) What can each person offer—areas of expertise and interest?
5) What is each person's availability for in-person assistance?
6) What is each person's tech-savvy level?
7) What resources are available already, and what needs to be secured?
8) What are the time limitations for each Care Team member?
9) What is each person's comfort level and availability for responsiveness?

1) Who needs to be included in the communications?

Each family member may choose to play a role of some sort in the Care Team or not. In some families, the role they choose is to do nothing. We all hope things with family will be fair and equitable and make sense. They don't.

The sibling of my friend T disappeared from his family. No contact at all. He didn't want to know what was happening, offered no help to their parents, and was not interested. He said, "Do not contact me again." Ouch! When their dad declared, "But I want to divide all my assets equally," this decision was made even though T was taking her dad and mom to doctors, packing up their belongings, moving them to assisted living when needed, burying their mom when that happened, grocery shopping and errands, and more. Further pain erupted when Dad didn't want to acknowledge his grandkids (his daughter's children) in his Will when the kids spent every holiday with him, and he was joining them at their house for dinners and meeting their partners. If being a caregiver for you is about recognition for your selflessness, you're going to have a hard time reconciling the possible harsh reality.

Some caregivers want to know everything and be involved in every step; others prefer to have the bird's-eye view and want to be informed generally, asking you to reach out when something "important" needs to be adopted (usually that means financial or medical decisions).

The communication plan might involve people considered family but not by blood. Outside the family may be advisors who play a role in how the family functions. These may be household help, medical team, financial advisors, neighbors, business or household managers, etc.

Please list all the people who need to know when changes have been made because it impacts them on some level. You might have the A-list for those who get all the info and the B-list that gets specific info relevant to that group. Think of it like Facebook, where you choose Friends Only or public postings.

2) **How often does information need to be shared?**

I began by sharing information daily with my family while selling my parent's New York apartment. In Florida, the information came weekly, and then, as things with my parents settled into a routine, I sent communication every few weeks, eventually reduced to monthly updates or when something urgent occurred. As my dad's physical health worsened and my mom had health emergencies, the frequency increased to daily at some points. Since I am a writer, it was more comfortable for me to text/email. My schedule was so haphazard that writing emails at 11 p.m. before bed or 7 a.m. when I woke or between doctor visits was easier than trying to get everyone on a call. Most importantly, this written content also served as the record of everything, so any one of us could take over if need be.

Some people prefer less frequent communication or maybe on an as-needed basis only. The only thing that is for sure is that you all must agree on what is expected going forward regarding frequency, level of detail, and the kind of content to include.

My truth is that I always had a fear that if something were to happen to me, I would not want my family to be overwhelmed and confused. I would not want my siblings to feel they couldn't pick up and continue caring for my parents while I was unavailable. When that free world cruise fell into my lap (I was entering every sweepstakes I could), I wanted the transition to be seamless. Knowing the world wouldn't fall apart if I was not in charge anymore was a relief.

Sure enough, when I was diagnosed with a rare eye cancer and needed to take care of myself, I asked my siblings to help out with our mom. It was not the cruise I had hoped for but we were ready. No questions were asked as my sister flew to Florida and cared for Mom and me when I had treatment to go through. I did not have to worry about bringing Dawn up to date while I was in the hospital undergoing surgery, radiation, and recovery.

We can't plan everything that will happen in life, so the best we can do is make sure that we have made it easier to manage when the unexpected arises. This keeps the stress level down a hundred notches.

3) **What kind of communication is preferred?**

The options for communication are plentiful. The primary phone call works but consider making it a conference call if you have a group. The conference call function is easy to use on a smartphone and keeps you from repeating yourself multiple times. Phones work for people/families who like to discuss everything.

The most basic but slower form of communication that's been around the longest is the old-fashioned letter sent by mail. Handwritten or typed, an actual letter is always welcomed more than bills in the mail. Back in the day (when I was but a wee girl), I made family newsletters and sent them to relatives every quarter.

A web meeting with images of everyone (Zoom, Google Teams, and Webex are examples of current providers for this service) allows people to see each other, and there is a share screen option if documents or images need to be reviewed by a few people at once.

If you choose a video or audio recording, you can have it transcribed to be available for the person in your family who prefers to read information. You can use Otter.ai or other services to record and transcribe every call or group meeting. The follow-up notes separate out the speakers and identifies key points and follow-up actions to take.

There are a few web options for publicly sharing someone's health status when multiple people need to be kept in the loop. You can use something like CaringBridge.com to post updates for the public or create a private invited list. This is a great time and energy saver if you update people on a surgery, hospital stay, treatment regimen, etc., so you don't have to repeatedly answer the same questions. People can post their well wishes and comments for you to share with the patient. People can volunteer to help or be a companion or offer respite. These sites can also be used for fundraising if your loved one needs help with bills.

Just because I like to write doesn't mean I couldn't share via video postings or audio recordings. What is your personal preference? Then, ask what everyone else on the care team's preferences are. My brother is on the phone all day and finds text messages annoying, preferring calls or email. My sister is on the go and prefers texts for urgent issues and emails otherwise. My mother loves to talk and prefers phone calls or Facetime. So, I have done a combination of these depending on what is happening and the urgency.

I like having things in writing because it creates a searchable history. I put my appointments with name, address, and phone number in my calendar. I can search emails for target words. It is not as easy to do in a series of videos or audio unless you use the latest AI (artificial intelligence) tech. AI allows you to record a meeting via video or audio, transcribing everything so it's searchable.

When a doctor asks, "When was his last MRI?" I go to the operating system magnifying glass and search "MRI," all the communication and documents that include MRI pop up. It could be an email, in my calendar, a journal entry, or a letter I wrote. It's all there.

If I need to remember the name of the person we met with about some legal issues and I'm having my own "senior moment" or "brain fart," I can search for the keywords on the topic, and the name will be included. Same thing if everything is in Word or Pages documents. Text messages are complex unless you regularly download and save the text transcripts.

The decision you make on communication style can evolve. It does not have to remain a static choice. After Dad passed away, I wanted to be sure Mom was okay without aides coming daily. My siblings wanted to know what was happening with Mom, too. We asked Mom to text our family members (she labeled our phone group "My Kids") every morning to let us know she was up and about. We'd respond with a thumbs-up or heart emoji. Over time, Mom started including her day's schedule. I added my big tasks for the day related to family caregiving. Thus, the email updates became less cumbersome and frequent, and the texts kept us all in the loop. But they're not searchable.

4) What can each person offer in areas of expertise and interest?

My brother is an IT guy and hooked up the living room video camera so we could watch Dad because he was prone to falling. My brother is also on the computer and in and out of bank stuff all day for his business. He was able to handle payroll for the aides while I was out of town and away from the internet. My brother fixes Mom's iPhone or computer issues. He explained the tablet and how to transition from solitaire with a deck of cards to using game programs for Dad. My brother is the go-to guy for special deals and pricing comparisons. He's so good at that.

My sister's kids are grown and out of the house. She works part-time and volunteers for various causes, giving her a flexible schedule. She helped me by ordering things Mom needed and shipping them straight to Mom's door. When Mom complained about her office chair, a new one appeared at the apartment. When my parents moved and needed new beds, my sister researched hospital beds, ordered them, and had them delivered to the new apartment. Taking all that research and shopping off my own to-do list was a huge relief.

Asking my mom to text my sister instead of me meant that I was not bombarded all day with random notes like "mayonnaise," "Metamucil wafers (on sale at Costco)," "leather belt size 44," etc. This freed up my mental space. My sister has patience and logic, can talk to Mom for an hour, and encourage her to organize her paperwork and home. Sis was able to research all the Age-in-Place communities in our area of Florida and narrow down choices for me to visit in person. On my sister's next visit to Florida, we narrowed the choices to three places to take my parents to see.

My sister and brother would try to come to Florida (before the pandemic changed everything) alternating months offering themselves anywhere from a weekend to a whole week to give me a break so I could go away or handle my errands and tasks. A blessing beyond words. And even when COVID was happening, my sis and brother allowed me to take a stay-at-home writing retreat by taking on the daily calls with Mom and Dad. If there was something I needed to handle, a crisis, I was still in town, and they knew how to reach me.

Who is good at what in your family? My friend M's brother is affluent but too busy to support their mother's care daily. He sends the funds that allow their mother to live in a better community with nurses and aides, so the burden isn't all on my friend. My friend lives in their mother's house, and both brothers pay the bills for unplanned expenses like a roof leak, hurricane damage, or torn lanai screen. She is grateful for having her brothers as care partners. They have family meetings via conference calls to share updates on their mother's status.

I have found that everyone has something they can contribute. If not from a business background, from life experiences. Can you divide up the areas of your loved one's life and assign people a way to be involved? It might be time (companionship), technology, finance, bill paying, health, wellness, errand running, construction/handyperson and home responsibilities, driving or car care, pet care, food supply/cooking, travel, etc.

When you need aides or nursing care, can someone interview, hire, and supervise the people while another handles payroll and administration issues? One person can drive for errands, and another can come by to provide a home mani/pedi or grooming day for your mutual loved one. I remember those days of clipping Dad's gnarly toenails. Reading a book or watching a movie with a loved one is as valuable as monitoring medicines or balancing the checkbook.

When you come together for an updated report, everyone will have something to contribute, and no one will feel that all the responsibility is exclusively on them. Plus, no one gets all the credit for caregiving. Spread the good karma all around.

5) What is each person's availability for in-person assistance?

Whether everyone lives in the same neighborhood or people are scattered around the world, who can be there, and when are they available? What time zones are you dealing with? When can everyone gather, and how often? Communication should be done so that people can access it when they are available and able to concentrate. Three in the afternoon in my time zone might be three in the morning in yours; that usually doesn't work for a Zoom session.

Consider using a group calendar to know when each person is coming in for care duty and what slots need to be filled. There are calendars on most smartphones that can be shared with multiple users.

Outlook, Google Teams, Basecamp, Slack, and Evernote are well known programs that offer shared calendars. My mother and I share a calendar on our iPhones that I named "Car Schedule." This began as appointments that required at least one of us to travel but evolved into anything we both needed to know.

Search for "remote workgroups" or "collaboration tools" in your browser to find an assortment of options available for free or small fees that will allow you to create a project for your family/caregiving group. You can use these programs to:

- ❖ Create a task/to-do list and assign each item to a specific person with a deadline. When the task is completed, they can check it off without having to contact anyone, and you'll all know it's been taken care of.
- ❖ You can share documents, reports, images, and files to mutually review and update as needed.
- ❖ Insert or review appointments with assignments on who does what with whom and when.
- ❖ You can even create a shared shopping list so when one of the Care Team members is at the market or the hardware store or shopping online at 3 a.m., they can look at the list and mark it off as "purchased," so there won't be duplicate purchases.

When everyone on the caregiving team is busy and has their own life going on, having a way to organize caregiving can provide documentation and tracking to ensure nothing falls through the cracks. It provides, at least for me, a breathing space because I don't have to rely on my memory to recall what I said I would do and when I said it would be done. It's right there at my fingertips to look it up.

Using a workgroup program or shared calendar becomes a great accountability tool. You won't get into the "but you said you were doing that" arguments when "that" wasn't completed.

Plus, with scheduled response/completion dates clearly stated, everyone has an opportunity to renegotiate if their personal life has some bumps or schedule conflicts.

6) **What is each person's tech-savvy level?**

Most people under fifty years old are comfortable with smartphones and computers. That doesn't mean that everyone knows the same software or functionality. Before assuming everyone is on board, ensure the entire Care Team is comfortable with whatever programs you use and can access them on their own devices.

Once you add people who are not daily computer users, you'll want to ensure some training is offered to be sure they are comfortable with your communication processes and systems. Further in this book are some tips to help with education.

If I use Mail on my iPhone or you use Outlook or Google on your android, if I have a Mac and you have a PC, if I speak in text and you prefer email, we must agree on what will work best that functions in all systems. If someone has only a home answering machine and you're leaving voice mail on cell phones, someone will miss important information and feel left out. Back to the basics of this book—it's all about communication.

7) **What resources are available already, and what needs to be secured?**

Once you've assessed the safety of your loved one's physical space and then completed a cognitive assessment of their emotional and mental capacity to manage their surroundings and responsibilities, you will have generated a list of things that need to be done, decisions that must be made, resources that will be required, and eventually a budget for all. Who already has what is needed? Who has access to what needs to be procured? What needs to be researched, sourced, and secured? Who will do each?

Save time and energy (and perhaps money) by reaching out to people you know to source what's needed. Who might have access to something on the list to whom you can delegate or make a request?

I had a friend who happened to be moving (which I didn't know beforehand). I posted my need for a piece of exercise equipment so I could work out at home thus being more accessible while caring for my parents, and she called me with a free treadmill!

Another day, I reached out to my network for a wheelchair and received a free chair from a fellow caregiver in my support group. Her mother was moved to assisted living and no longer needed the chair.

It doesn't hurt to ask. Being prepared with a list in advance of the need for certain items means less stress and allows you to save money before you have to find them last minute.

8) **What are the time limitations for each family member?**

My brother committed to handling payroll for my parents' aides while I was on a trip. It turns out that his business got in the way of the last week of his doing that, and I got a text from one aide that she wasn't paid. This time, it was not a disaster because I was within range of the internet and could handle it.

This teaches us that knowing what everyone's time limitations are in advance will help when delegating responsibilities. Best intentions are great but can lead to more issues if things aren't completed. Agree to be honest with each other about what works and doesn't. I say yes to too many things and then scramble. Wouldn't I be more intelligent to say no when it's too much? Yes. But we caregiver types tend to want to help everyone and be the can-do folks. I'm learning. Take a lesson from me.

Find out if people are more available during the week, days or nights, or weekends only. Are they available only on vacation, or it's a national holiday, and the business is closed for the day? Can they work during their insomnia hours but not while kids are awake and needing attention?

Can they only do things when it's added to their existing schedule? Like running errands for you when they're already out at the supermarket, hardware store, drug store, dog park, picking up take-out, etc. Maybe they can add cooking for your loved one when they're already cooking for a family at home by just making extra and packing it up in a container or zippered pouch or freezing a bunch of stuff to load the freezer at your loved one's home.

Delegating is easier if you do a simple survey of all the people who can be a resource, and finding out how to reach them makes it easier for them to say yes.

I have used Google Surveys or Survey Monkey programs (but there are others) to create surveys I can email to a group of people. When people respond, their answers are automatically compiled, and I know who is available when, who can/wants to do what, and where I have gaps. Whew! That takes a burden off me because I won't have to start anew with each task/project trying to figure out who has an interest and availability to help.

My advice is to make use of the tech and web resources that are available these days to make your life easier. Search "digital assistant" to find out what's available and get more ideas on how to use these tools.

9) What is each person's comfort level and availability for responsiveness?

Setting agreements for responsiveness

A crucial part of all of this is that people do what they say they're going to do, when they promised.

My mother and brother have the same responsiveness reaction. If they send me a text, I should respond almost immediately. If I don't, I will get follow-up texts: *Are you alive? Did you get my text? What's going on?* However, if I send a text to either of them, they don't have any problem taking a day or longer to respond because it is not a priority to them. So, as my therapist would caution, you can't believe you're unimportant because they don't respond. They have a different processing system for responding. Finding out what works for each person will help keep you sane!

The corporate CEO, truck driver, police officer, or sports coach might not look at their phone or email all day. Some jobs might not allow for interruptions or distractions. You wouldn't expect a doctor in the middle of surgery to answer your call or text you back, right? Whereas someone who works from home, is caregiving full time, or otherwise has time between appointments to check emails or texts can respond more proactively. Asking ahead of time about how someone responds helps you plan accordingly.

Knowing if someone responds more readily to phone, text, or email will help you plan. My mother says, "Text me, and if I don't respond, then call me." My nieces and nephews exclusively answer texts. My medical team asked me to email them. After all, email is on their phones/tablets. My lawyer prefers me to leave a voice mail with details, and they will respond by or at the end of the business day. Why get myself frustrated by sending my request in the wrong format? Note the preferred method for each person on the contact page of your smartphone, so you have a quick way to refer back and not rely on memory.

If there's an emergency, it helps to have a Care Team code that lets people know, "This is critical. Stop what you're doing and call me back immediately." My family uses a text code number and instructions on who to call: "9-1-1 Call Mom." If one of us receives that in a text message, we react.

A final option is to have a written agreement about what is expected. Something like:

> *I, [insert name], agree to respond within [fill in duration] hours to your message regarding our (fill in relationship with caree—mother, father, parents, cousin, child, sister, etc.) or (name of caree) unless you advise me otherwise.*

The detail level of this little agreement can get quite deep with customized consequences for non-responding or specifics about what must be included in the message, the format the message is to be sent, etc. It's up to you and your comfort level with each person to customize this.

Use tech whether you choose to go with a written agreement or not. Please ask and learn what people want. It is the only way to create a more cohesive support network for caregiving.

FRIENDS AND NEIGHBORS

For those people who live and work in the same community where they were raised and went to school, you are probably surrounded by a support network to help with caregiving. You have your village.

When raising children in a community, you get to know other parents through school events, parent/teacher events, or after-school recreational activities. It creates bonds and a network of people you can share responsibilities with and count on in emergencies.

Suppose you live in the same community where all your family still live, moved to a gated community, belong to clubs and organizations, or attend religious services. In that case, you can create a network of friends, family, and neighbors who want to help you if you're faced with a crisis.

But what about those who perhaps moved to another location to provide caregiving and are isolated from everyone they ever knew? What about those who are shy and don't easily make friends? What about the people who feel like asking for help is a sign of weakness or makes them uncomfortable? Creating and activating a support network is not easy for all these people. I get it. Here are some tips I learned as an ambivert (mixture of extrovert and introvert), forcing myself to create a new village in Florida to support me in caring for my parents.

Finding Your People

Support Group

Attending a local support group is the best place to start finding or creating your village. Make the time. Whether virtual or on-site, you will meet people who can offer tips to keep your life more manageable and local resources to make things happen when you feel like the brakes are on and you're stuck. Support group friends keep you from feeling like you're going crazy when you just need to vent and get it all off your chest.

Fellow caregivers can also share responsibilities with you, like parents share child-raising duties. Mutually beneficial collaboration includes:

- ❖ Carpooling – I'll drive our moms to bingo at the senior center today; you drive them tomorrow.
- ❖ Errand running – I'll pick up your pre-ordered groceries if you can get my dad from adult daycare. I'll drop off your groceries when I pick up Dad at your place.
- ❖ Activities – Drop your mom off at my place, and our moms can watch movies together so you can get a haircut. I'll drop my mom off at your place next week so I can treat myself to coffee with an old friend who will be in town.

Community Activity

Find something that is just for you. Something that lifts you, makes you happy, gives you energy, brings a smile to your face. And then do that with other people who feel the same way. Whether it's worship, creative arts (singing, writing, acting, sculpting, filming), movement/dance/exercise, reading, or movies—whatever—you will make friends doing these things, and they will want to help you because you have much in common.

Additional Resources

- Reach out to volunteer organizations that offer free help to the community.
- Ask the local schools or houses of worship if they have students looking for service credits and see if someone gets along with your loved one to be a companion or help you with errands.
- Contact local chapters of support: elder advisors, cancer care, Alzheimer's support, or whatever else has brought you into the caregiving role. These organizations should have advice, resources, volunteers, and contacts for you.
- Get to know the neighbors. Let them know you're caregiving and would appreciate them keeping an eye out. If you can share keys and have people available to talk with, that will help grow the network of people able to support you.
- People who know your loved one and already care for them may offer their assistance once you introduce yourself, so reach out and make an effort to invite them in.

EXPERTS/PROFESSIONALS TO ADD TO THE CARE TEAM

In addition to your loved one's family and close contacts, you might find that certain professionals included in your Care Team can help you avoid costly mistakes with missed opportunities, deadlines, documents, etc.

These advisors might be on call when a question or need arises. Having people familiar with the specific estate and wishes of your loved one can save time and keep information relevant. Dr. Google or Google Esq is not the place you want to rely on for your most critical caregiving decision-making.

Advisors don't need to be part of every decision or communication. They probably wouldn't want that at all. But sending them updates relevant to their area of expertise to add to the file is a great way to ensure continuity of care no matter who takes the lead.

For example, if moving to a continuing care community means that you will be selling a home, packing, and relocating, the legal and financial advisors should be part of that, in addition to the real estate people you need. But then you also must let the banks, doctors, and VA (for a veteran) know about your change of address. All the new expenses will impact financial status. Legal documents need to be updated with the current address, and perhaps new documents drafted that evolve with changes in care or competency, and so on.

Who you might include on your Care Team depends on the complexities of a person's life. Some typical advisors for your consideration:

- Lawyer
- Physicians
- Financial Advisors
- CPA, Bookkeeper, Financial Concierge
- Household/Property Managers
- Veterans Administration Contact
- Elder Care Advisor
- Real Estate Manager or Broker

Additionally, you might find certain people with areas of expertise and resource management that would be good to have on speed dial for local support. Some examples:

- Pet Care (veterinarian, dog walker, pet sitter, cat feeder, etc.)
- Pharmacist
- Medical Supply Store Manager or Salesperson
- Home Care Providers (aides, nurses, companion care)
- Drivers and Transportation (taxi, medical transport, handicapped/senior bus service)

This list of critical contacts should be made available to everyone in your care team. Whether it's posting it in your project software or simply sending a list monthly or quarterly to everyone on the care team, keeping the contents current will ensure that if something happened to you, the others could still manage the care of your loved one.

If you are not the primary caregiver, you might want to ask for this list from the person handling the day-to-day care so you can follow up in a pinch without scrambling to find this information.

SUPPORT GROUP

One of the most essential things for your well-being as a caregiver is having a network of people to turn to for advice, listen to you vent, and share in your journey. Your group could be ad hoc, or you might want people facing similar challenges. I went to several caregiver support groups around my area until I found the one with people I could relate to. I wanted people caring for parents versus those caring for spouses or kids. I didn't need a caregiver group focused on cancer patients, so I went to a memory care center because I knew my dad's Alzheimer's would be the bulk of my responsibilities. My caregiving support group made sharing my feelings about what I was going through easier by knowing that everyone in the room understood what I meant and could, on some level, relate to my challenges.

I found support groups essential to keeping me centered. Similar to twelve-step programs like Alcoholics Anonymous or Narcotics Anonymous meetings, things are kept private in support groups. People are encouraged to respect each other's experiences without judging. The goal of these meetings is the freedom to share. The group will fall apart when someone decides that one person's experience is invalid or less important than another's. When a professional facilitator leads the group, that kind of judgment and denigration is not likely to happen.

These groups might meet weekly, biweekly, or monthly. They might be local and meet in a regular location or virtual and meet via conference software. Most are free, but some might have a small cost attached to pay for the facilitator. While many of these groups are hosted by health establishments or nonprofits, it is my hope that over time more places will offer time and space to meet at your workplace or house of worship or community organization.

Communication within the support group may be very structured, with people registering for a specified period (i.e., twelve weeks) with the same people attending each week for the series. Or it may be unstructured, where people wander in and out of the group, week by week, by invitation of current active members or the host organization. Meetings may be held virtually, in a conference room, rotating homes, restaurants, or parks. There may be an education component followed by discussion or a more informal go-around-the-table sharing format.

Be creative and find nonjudgmental people who will offer you a way to share and learn. Self-constructed support groups may take place in all sorts of formats. It may be a coffee break after a yoga class, a book club, a walking group, a wine meet-up at a bar/restaurant, or a weekly cooking session in rotating kitchens. Support comes from a connection to people who matter to you and to whom you matter.

Suppose you hold everything inside because you're stoic or believe you don't have time for talking. In that case, you might be heading into burnout, defeatism, or active resentment of your loved ones and the person you're caring for. No one wants to get to that point. Believe me!

Part 4
COMMUNICATION IN THE TECHNOLOGY AGE

Apps
Social Media
Tablets
Smartphones
Computers

COMMUNICATING IN THE TECHNOLOGY AGE

Thanks to the internet and digital technology advances, some incredible resources have been created to maximize the benefits of your devices, making your caregiving life more manageable and enhancing communication opportunities between Care Team members. New apps are being developed daily. To list them all here would be a monumental task and possibly out of date by the time you read this. I've mentioned some specific programs I like in the previous chapters.

Here are some keywords to use in a search browser to find current devices, tech, and apps to address your caregiving challenges.

- Caregiving Team, Care Team, Caregiver Resources, Caregiver Organizations
- Collaboration Tools, Project Management Tools, Workgroup Tools
- Patient Website, Patient Advocate, Patient Navigator
- Shared Calendar, Scheduling Tools
- Time Management Tools
- Password Management Tools
- Digital Document Storage, Digital Vault, Digital Estate
- Crowd Funding For... Healthcare/Disease/Medical Expenses
- Eldercare Organizations (Insert Local City), Senior Services In (Insert City/Town)
- Ride Services For Seniors
- Handicapped, Medical Transport
- Adult Day Program Near Me

Social Media

If you don't have a Care Team, if you feel isolated and are struggling to do it all on your own, social media has enabled the whole world—or a limited world, if you choose—to see what's going on in your life. It also gives you a chance to reach out and ask for assistance for a day/week/month/project/task/financial aid to cover a cost or to find a network of people who can provide support when you feel alone and disconnected.

Millions of people worldwide are going through what you are doing right now. Someone is online waiting to connect with you! The most common social media sites (at this writing: Facebook, WhatsApp, Instagram, YouTube) allow you to reach larger audiences to hear your story, or you can find others with whom you can empathize. Each one works differently. Find the ones that make you feel comfortable and join a group of like-minded souls who can offer advice and suggestions when you have a challenge, and ears or eyes to watch and listen when you want to share. You'll learn that you're not alone.

Check out life and caregiving tips and tricks on TikTok. Head to LinkedIn to find professionals who offer the services you require, and when you're ready to enter the workforce, look for mentors and potential job openings.

Neighborhood-centered platforms (i.e., NextDoor, Front Porch Forum, Freecycle, EveryBlock, and Patch—all in the US) offer places to post volunteer opportunities and goods to donate or to request. You can ask for what you need from your local area neighbors, and someone you don't even know might have just the help you need or want things that you are ready to let go of.

Devices

Using a smartphone or a tablet can help you stay in touch with your loved one. Someone who insists on living in their home by themselves won't feel so isolated if you and others check in through video chat. Providing these gadgets in the versions designed for seniors or young children means larger keypads, simple instructions, and limited functionality to learn, which makes it appealing to any technophobe. Look for them on sale around holiday times.

Computers can be very advanced, but they have also been brought down to simple versions with inexpensive pricing to make them more accessible. Refurbished models and older platforms are much less expensive than the new, shiny versions, but work equally well. Computers can help your loved ones and the whole Care Team stay in touch and educated. Ask your local tech geek for recommendations that will work with what your Care Team and loved one need.

If the tech stuff is financially out of reach:

- ❖ Libraries offer free use of computers and usually have trainers and classes.
- ❖ Local high schools and colleges have beginner classes and may have donated equipment to lend or provide.
- ❖ Consider starting a crowdfunding page to let strangers underwrite the cost for you. The website GoFundMe.com has practical, easy-to-understand information on how to do this.
- ❖ Look for local nonprofits that offer devices on loan, through grants, or re-distribution of older donated items.
- ❖ One of your neighbors may have purchased an updated device and doesn't need their older model any longer. They might be happy to find a good home for a still-functional device and avoid sending it to the tech landfill. (Check Facebook Marketplace, NextDoor, Craig's List, etc.)

Note: Consider including a gift card for a local tech geek or trainer to instruct your loved one on using new devices or apps until they feel comfortable.

VIDEO ETIQUETTE

Beginning in 2020, thanks to COVID-19 forced isolation, we suddenly became aware of all the ways to communicate with people when you can't be in the same room. The tech I watched on *The Jetsons* animated show as a child turned out to be the savior of a pandemic-stricken twenty-first-century global community.

COVID-19 created and expanded the market for group teleconferencing, video phone calls, and conference calls with multiple people from all over the globe on the same call. Emailing, texting, and instant messaging services have become even more valuable than before, not just for business use. The internet has now made long-distance calls to different countries affordable. All these tools are now invaluable to families and friends who want to see and talk to each other when health or distance makes it a challenge.

I attended several funerals and memorials via Zoom. I have friends who attended weddings. I know of a bar mitzvah that was broadcast on Zoom. I hosted my father's Celebration of Life in a multi-purpose room where he lived and via Zoom so his extended family and friends from around the country could participate. The truth is that before the technology came along, family members residing a plane distance away wouldn't usually come in for these events. Now we can have a reunion and catch up. It is remarkable how far we've come.

Naturally, with a learning curve, new tech users made some gaffs and flubs. Baffled, confused technophobes reached out to the young people in their network for help, creating new bonds between old and young. And, like everything else in a civilized society (such as we are), there eventually come unwritten and delineated etiquette updates for tech users. People familiar with technology need to release assumptions when talking with retired people who may have no experience with technology and will require some patience for the learning curve.

After an entire family Zoom holiday gathering with my mother's knee filling the camera lens and a community board meeting where we listened to the clang of a dinner table being set because someone forgot to mute themselves, I put together a list of tips for my family and friends to share with their families for the video conferencing sessions we all now attend.

Google Meet, WebEx, and Zoom are top-rated visual gathering programs, and (as of this writing) all offer free versions. There are more professional applications that corporations use for secure meetings. With people meeting their doctors for telehealth and virtual gatherings for anything from book clubs and quilting to play dates and dating, learning etiquette for virtual gatherings is polite and necessary.

DIRTY DOZEN VIDEO CONFERENCE GATHERING ETIQUETTE AND TIPS

1) **Assign a leader.** If you have more than two to four people in your group video session, I recommend appointing a leader to keep things moving. The leader can:

    ❖ Introduce the purpose of the call.
    ❖ Introduce each person (and perhaps invite individuals to share more about who they are if new to the group).
    ❖ Call on people to share the info or stories that everyone has gathered to hear, as we each see the tiles of faces in different order.
    ❖ Monitor the time each participant gets to speak so no one monopolizes the whole conversation or interrupts with stories they want to share to the detriment of others being able to speak.

2) **Test your technology** before the meeting begins.

    ❖ Log in early to the meeting link sent in the invitation to use the Test audio/Test video functions before the gathering begins.
    ❖ When you log in through the invite link, the software will load whatever you need (usually, it's taking you to the website for the meeting), and you can "accept" when it asks if you want to "allow this on your computer."
    ❖ You may be asked to submit a password, which would have been included in the invitation.
    ❖ If you don't have a video (or don't feel like putting on clothing!) or are driving, you can join via telephone—without the video. Instructions to call in are usually on the invite.

3) **Familiarize yourself with the meeting controls.** Before the meeting gets going, look at the controls along the bottom and top of the screen to learn how you can change the view of the people speaking in the meeting, how to mute, turn on/off the video image of yourself, ask a question in the chat area, share your screen, etc.

    You can see everyone on the screen at once (like *The Brady Bunch* theme tiles) or have people across the top or side and the current speaker enlarged in the center of your screen. Know that sometimes the speaker (in a seminar, for example) will control what and how you see what's on the screen, perhaps posting slides or text to help illustrate the speaker's points.

> Note: This is what it looks like in Room Meeting Controls when you've muted your audio (no one can hear you or anything happening around you) and your video (in case there is a lot of activity behind you or you don't feel like being seen).
>
>

4) **Be on time**. If you're late, join in mute mode to avoid disturbing the current speaker.

5) **Frame the camera correctly:**

    ❖ Look at yourself and make sure the viewers can see your whole face (not just your eyes, mouth, up your nose—don't ask!—the ceiling, or the background).
    ❖ Angle the camera so there's no reflection in your glasses; we need to see your eyes!

6) **Check the lighting**. Please don't sit in front of a window or light; we only see your silhouette. The light should illuminate your face. Move a lamp in front of you if needed.

> **Note**: The web offers many inexpensive versions of a Ring Light that will stand on the table/desk, hold your phone/camera still, and illuminate your face if a bright background is your only option and you can't put your face toward the light.

It helps to be where there's not too much happening in the background. Please keep it simple.

> **Note**: Talk to a tech geek or do a web search for instructions on changing the background. You can put yourself in front of a beach, the moon, a garden, or a wide assortment of screen backgrounds to block distractions, clutter, or personal belongings behind you.

7) **Look into the camera**. We tend to direct our eyes to the images of people on the screen. Still, the camera is centered at the top of your computer screen, so make the people's images large enough so you are facing the camera and not looking down or off to the side when you're talking.

8) **Mute yourself when you're not speaking**. We don't need to hear the TV your partner watches in the other room, the upstairs neighbors on the treadmill, or family or pets having fun in the background. We prefer not to watch you eat, hear the clink of your spoon as you stir your coffee,

or hear a chip bag crackling. In summary, every time you move, we all hear those noises unless you mute your microphone when you're not speaking. Thanks!

9) **Wait your turn**. There's nothing more aggravating than one person monopolizing the conversation or interrupting everyone else. On Zoom, a yellow box highlights the person currently speaking. You can watch the light to see who's "got the mic," so to speak. You can raise/wave your hand if you have something to add and thus will be acknowledged. You can use the chat function (see below) to notate something you want to add or say without interrupting.

10) **Pay attention**. Answering texts and phone messages and responding to emails while in the group session is rude, just like it would be if we were talking in person. So, if you need to handle something, turn off your microphone and video so we know you're otherwise occupied for a moment.

11) **Utilize the chat area**. You can send a note to someone individually or a question to everyone on the call from the chat area, like raising your hand in a classroom. You'll notice the chat icon flashing, or it will have a number when there are messages from someone else in the meeting. This is where people usually put extra info like phone numbers or links to things being discussed in the group.

One caution: If someone sends the transcription of the chat area to the group after the gathering, your private messages to someone *will* be included. Please don't make fun of people or say nasty things because others will be able to see it afterward.

12) **Remember, you are in public!** People forget that they have a video on and have done some things that should be done privately. For example, please do *not* take us all into the bathroom with you! Ensure the camera is not facing a bathroom behind you, where other people may conduct their private business. If you are exercising while talking (I admit I do this), keep the image steady so the other participants aren't seasick. These may be funny notes to read, but check YouTube, and you'll see plenty of stories about these kinds of faux pas because we forget we have a video camera in our hands.

Part 5

GENERAL CONVERSATION TIPS

SELF-CARE VS. THE GLOOM AND DOOM REPORTERS

You've settled in with a nice hot cuppa something, and you're looking forward to reading the paper or listening to a podcast when you get a call. You look at the caller ID, your eyes raise to the ceiling, and you go through an internal self-check before deciding if you will answer the call: "Do I have the patience to talk to X right now?" "Can I handle negativity today?" "How long do I have before I have to be somewhere?" If you answer the call, you will be dragged into the gossip of the neighborhood/building/community/office. You know you will hear everything wrong, whether it's weather, personal health, politics, or general societal issues. Maybe it's not the right time, so you let the call go to voice mail.

I have a friend who is a genuinely good person. She was the caregiver for her husband, who was a wheelchair user and had cognitive decline issues. She's now a retired lawyer, but while she was still working, I was witness to her office problems, the decline and passing of her husband, a few hip, knee, and other surgeries, her case of COVID, and the entire cycle of real estate (selling a house, finding a rental, moving to the new rental). I can tell you all the stories of her neighbors, kids, and professionals she engaged along the way, as well as her client's ups and downs (but not the details of their cases, of course) and her travel adventures. I can't say that she would be able to give you very much information about me because after, "So, how are you?" and my "Pretty good" response, I could literally put the phone down, run errands, and come back, and she wouldn't have paused to see if I was still listening. As much as I love her, I didn't take her calls unless I had a lot of free time.

When my friend asked how my parents were and then interrupted my response to tell me a worse medical story or a similar friend story, I found myself disconnecting and saying, "Whoops, got another call coming in. Gotta take this. Bye." That's certainly an option.

I now recognize that people like my friend (and my mother) are not necessarily trying to dump on me. They need to talk. They are lonely. They may be unburdened by simply sharing. They may arrive at the next step or solution to a problem by hearing themselves speak. So, does that mean it's my job to listen? I don't need to get sucked into what I recognize as an auditory abuse cycle. I can choose how to react, respond, and follow up for the sake of the caller and my current health and well-being.

There are ways to divert the conversation back to being give and take. You are obligated to yourself, for your own care, to leave conversations that get you too depressed, angry, and anxious. We all know the Negative Nellies and Nasty Neds out there. It may be their choice to relieve stress by unloading on you, but it is up to us whether we want to absorb it. I can't help feeling that if you're gossiping or raging about others to me, what are you saying about me to others?

Ways that we can be good supporters and turn things more positive include:

- ❖ **Empathizing** – Stating what you heard to show you've understood the issue.
- ❖ **Reframing** what they shared into a positive thing you could recognize them for, what they might have learned that will be useful in the future, or a new connection made because of the situation. "Everything happens for a reason, so let's figure out why you went through this and how it benefited you in the long run."
- ❖ **Divert** – Offer a possible resource or someone to help resolve the issue/complaint. That helps divert the follow-up to someone else and takes that off your plate.
- ❖ **Time Limit** – If the speaker needs to vent, you can acknowledge that but limit how long you must listen. "Hey, you probably need to vent and get this off your chest. I've got just five minutes, and then I've got to go. Tell me what's bothering you the most."
- ❖ **Create a Plan** – Change the time suck into something productive that values your contribution and raises your good karma because you were able to help. You might suggest, "I hear you. That is a tough challenge. How about we come up with a plan to resolve this? What are your next steps?" And then you won't get stuck in the negativity vortex of worsening issues the longer you listen.

My new favorite way of looking at things is, "Will this matter in a day? A week? A month? A year from now?" If the answer is no, why am I investing my time and energy in it? If I get a call and it's something I can do nothing about, then I should analyze why I'm staying engaged. It might go back to your need for approval, fear of people not liking you, and need to feel like you're helping. These questions are a way to refocus the storyteller.

You can always change a topic. When my mother starts telling me about the neighbor with glaucoma who lost an eye and is having a hard time, I stop her. "Mom, how's your vision?" or "How's Dad's catheter doing these days?" or something that gets the call focused back on the relevant things to me. I have limited time to spend on the phone or on a Facetime call. If I let Mom go on about the neighbor, I would soon hear the whole medical story and how that person's kids are treating this friend, and then I would get sucked into trying to help the neighbor find an aide, and soon I'd be negotiating with agencies on their behalf. That's how this has gone for me in the past. Is it any wonder that I experience caregiving burnout? I have to keep my energy up for the people I love. And, as my therapist keeps saying, I must learn to say *no*. Hmmm. That's not that easy for me, but I'm getting better at it because the alternative is me not being able to do anything for anyone at all when I crash and burn.

Setting boundaries for what is acceptable for you will keep your mental and emotional energy on the plus side and eliminate the damage energy vampires can do in your life.

CONVERSATION STARTERS FOR AGING LOVED ONES

When we visit with our loved ones, after the practical stuff is all resolved, we may find ourselves in a conversational dark hole with the person or people we care about. You've made it over to visit. How can you make use of the time you have together?

You may ask yourself, "What do I talk about now? We've run out of chitchat." What can you use as a conversation opener?

While someone is still conversant, you can have great conversations about someone's history, collecting life factoids and most-loved stories to prompt discussions later when your loved one seems despondent or lonely, has lost energy, or is trying to converse with a grandchild. If someone has mental cognition and memory issues, allowing them to tell stories they love to share can bring them out of their shell.

You might want to gather details of a life well-lived while sharing is still possible, store them, and then pull them up when needed to change a mood or motivate someone. You can use these facts and stories to distract someone in pain or bring someone back to your conversation if they become distracted by activities in the background.

To store these great stories, ask about a favorite activity with a grandchild, best memories with family, and lessons they want to teach children and grandchildren. What about favorite recipes that could be fun to pass down through generations? Maybe even write them down together in a journal or memory book. Or writing letters with advice (even decorating the envelopes) to children and grandchildren to be read at significant birthdays or life events (wedding day, graduation day, birth of a child, purchasing a home, etc.) Help your loved one feel like it is possible to remain part of family life even though they are aging.

Conversation Starters

- Where did you grow up?
- Who were your neighbors?
- Did you have a best friend?
- Did you have a nickname?
- What jobs did you have in your life?
- Where else have you lived?
- What are you most proud of in your life?
- What do you like to watch on TV? Sports? Movies? Cop shows? Documentaries?
- What are your favorite shows?
- Do you have a favorite radio show?
- What kind of music do you like?

- Who is your favorite singer?
- Who is your favorite movie star?
- What is your favorite movie?
- What books changed your life?
- What kind of books do you enjoy?
- What are your favorite hobbies?
- What kind of games do you like?
- Where was your favorite place to travel?
- Where have you traveled?
- Where do you wish you could go?
- What was your experience in the military like?
- What charities do you contribute to? Why?
- Have you ever belonged to any clubs?
- What is your favorite holiday? Why?
- Who was your favorite pet? Can you name all your pets?
- What is/was your favorite sport to play? Watch?
- What are your favorite foods?
- What is your favorite food to cook?
- Where do you like to go to relax (in the house, community, city, etc.)?

BE THE PROTECTOR

When you're a tiny child, you're oblivious to all the world's concerns because, ideally, your parents are there to shield you from anything that could harm you. You skip along, play with dirt, make new friends, and learn new skills through trial and error; every day is an adventure. Granted, not everyone lives in a Disney world of perfection, but youth has an innocence. In some communities and families, that innocence is lost early; in other situations, one might stay shielded until college graduation.

No matter what neighborhood or family dynamic you grew up in, that innocence returns for people in their supposed golden years. Due to mental, emotional, financial, or physical changes, our elderly must be watched and guided. Someone may take on the role of protector. Maybe that's you?

Two friends and I were reminiscing on the phone this week. They were telling me how being late-in-life mothers has put them in the role of caring for children in their early school years and getting their parents into and out of adult daycare. The Sandwich Generation. Caring for kids or adults is equally stressful but in different ways. Doing both is a monumental undertaking. Self-care is critical.

Every person has an image of how they want to be in this world. Wouldn't you want your family and friends to help you achieve your idea of a great day as often as possible? Our loved ones have an image of their great day. Soon, they may not remember what that is. In my opinion, through early and open communication, it is our role to learn what we need to know to help fulfill our parents' or loved ones' great days and last wishes. And to share our wishes and plans with loved ones who would be there for us.

I sincerely hope that the tools in this book have helped you figure out how to serve your loved ones in a way that brings you joy and fulfillment.

Fern Pessin   info@illberightthere.com   illberightthere.com

Content in this guidebook has been inspired by *I'll Be Right There: A Guidebook for Adults Caring for their Aging Parents* and *I'm Not Gonna Live Forever You Know: A Personal Archive for Sharing Your Wishes with Your Loved Ones*. Additional content was added. For more information or to purchase copies of the other books in the series, please visit http://www.illberightthere.com or your favorite bookseller. Email any questions to info@illberightthere.com.

Content included in *I'll Be Right There* and *I'm Not Gonna Live Forever You Know*:

- Behavioral Assessment
- Health Assessment
- Driving Assessment
- Mental, Cognitive, and Physical Decline
- Creating Expert Teams (Legal, Financial, Health, Household)
- Understanding Impairments (Multiple Stages)
- Helping People Stay at Home
- Hiring Caregivers
- Respite for Unpaid Caregivers
- Real Estate (Choosing New Home, Leaving Existing Home) Costs and Logistics
- End-of-Life Decisions
- Caregiver Support
- Worksheets and Forms for Health Tracking, Status and Resources, and Instructions to Family
- DNR/DNI and Life-Sustaining Measures
- Wellness Worksheets for Lifestyle and Comfort Wishes
- Worksheets for Financial Information and Resources
- Worksheets for Legal Information and Resources
- Home and Household Worksheets for Vendors, Schedules, Resources, Property, Neighbors
- Hiring and Managing Home Health Aide Worksheets
- End-of-Days Preferences and Prepaid Arrangements Worksheets

ACKNOWLEDGMENTS

I want to thank my mother (Hedda Pessin) not just for proofing my book and providing endless stories for me to include, but for her bravery as we finally confronted our lifelong relationship struggles. We have reached a new mutual level of respect and renewed love and affection. I toast to all the good ahead of us Mom!

My siblings have been my partners in managing our parents' health and home. I thank them for giving me the flexibility, trust, and recognition when I was full-time caregiving and for taking such great care of our mom after dad passed away when I needed to focus on healing the cancer that was invading my body.

I appreciate my siblings' spouses and children for being there to support Dawn and Mitch through this very emotional and often challenging time in all our lives.

Members of my caregiver support groups are mentioned throughout this book. I would not make it through any of this without them. Their feedback and input on my writings has been enlightening. I value their compassion and understanding, patience and humor.

Communication is the most essential tool any caregiver needs to have in the toolbox. I learn all I need from my fellow caregivers. From my caregiver support groups, to caregivers on all of the varied websites, in books and watching movies/television shows that share our challenging, emotional, journeys. I will continue to work towards employers, the public and government recognizing the valuable role caregivers play in our societal well-being and hope to see an evolution on policies that reflect that value.

To Sandra Grace Brooks, you were my heart and soul. You will be forever missed. Helping me to heal myself has allowed me to reach out into the world and help others.

To Jenn Grace and Niki Garcia at Publish Your Purpose Press, you guided me as a novice author and have led to me love writing and sharing with the public. Thank you for all your leadership, guidance, patience, and for generosity in answering my many questions over these last six plus years!

To the family O'Byrne... thank you for your help with birthing this book baby out into the world looking good!

To Denise, together we healed from loss. You have returned to me a zest for life, cooking, and exploring. You helped me carve a vision for the future, not just for me, but for global caregivers and the healthcare community. You introduced me to Julie and collectively we are creating a village of support. I look forward to all the adventures that lie ahead! Viva la Urban Villa!

FERN PESSIN BIO

In 2016, Fern Pessin left her consulting business in New York/Connecticut to move south to provide love and support for her parents' well-being as they aged. Surrounded by sunshine in Florida, Fern wanted to protect and maximize her parents' resources.

Fern used her skills as a writer, event planner, fundraiser, public relations, and promotion expert to learn what needed to be done to act as an advocate for her parents. She became certified as a home health aide, attended caregiver conferences and classes, read and watched materials, interviewed experts, and joined weekly support groups to ensure an understanding of what to look for and do for her parents both physically and emotionally. She collected a team of experts to guide her and her siblings through the financial, legal, and medical requirements of securing her parents' well-being over the long term. After some real lows, Fern learned the importance of creating a support village and recognized that self-care, setting boundaries, and asking for help was the only way she'd come out of her caregiving years intact.

Before relocating to Florida, Fern served on the board of Senior Services of Stamford, Connecticut (now Silver Source), where she used her skills to raise funds to help improve the quality of life for Fairfield County/Connecticut seniors and support their family caregivers. She also worked to raise millions of dollars for Alzheimer's disease organizations and cancer patients and their families at Bennett Cancer Center. Fern spent fifteen years as a consultant for the fitness industry, working to improve the quality of life for people of all ages.

Being a content contributor and expert column responder at Caregiving.com opened the doors for Fern to learn about the needs and questions of caregivers outside of her community. While visiting her parents in senior living communities, Fern talked with residents, their children, paid caregivers, and staff. Working with vendors has added additional perspective. Fern is now applying her skills, garnered over thirty years, to authoring books and creating support products and programs for caregivers and aging seniors.

From a caregiver's perspective and as an educator, writer, trainer, program designer, and international speaker, Fern is committed to illuminating ways for caregivers and their family members to find assistance, recognition, inspiration, and joy.

I'll Be Right There: A Guidebook for Adults Caring for their Aging Parents (2019) was written to remove the overwhelm of the caregiving role and support families on the caregiving journey by providing a road map with worksheets, schedules, and strategies.

I'm Not Gonna Live Forever, You Know: A Personal Archive for Sharing Your Wishes with Your Loved Ones (2023) is for anyone to communicate their wishes to people who care about them.

When Can We Talk? A Caregiver's Guidebook for Holding Discussions Around Difficult Topics (2023) guides families on having safe, loving, and productive conversations around difficult, uncomfortable, but essential topics. Fern's passion is to share communication strategies that help families peacefully make it through challenging experiences.

The Caregiver Gap Year: 12 Months to Grow, Aspire, and Explore all Possibilities After Caregiving Ends (2023), the final book in the caregiver support series, guides caregivers toward recovery after caregiving ends. How does one return to living for oneself after dedicating a huge chunk of time and resources toward caring for others? How does one create their optimal life? Whenever possible, the goal is to begin planning for post-caregiving years while still engaged in day-to-day caregiving.

Fern Pessin
www.illberightthere.com for regular blog posts, membership, courses, and books
info@illberightthere.com
Follow Fern Pessin, author, on Amazon to receive notice of the latest releases. FernOnAmazon.com
YouTube: @fernpessinIBRT
X: @IllBeRightTher1
Facebook: https://www.facebook.com/fernpessin

www.ingramcontent.com/pod-product-compliance
Lightning Source LLC
Chambersburg PA
CBHW080446110426
42743CB00016B/3292